TOASTER OVEN TAKEOVER

TOASTER OVEN TAKEOVER

EASY + DELICIOUS RECIPES TO MAKE IN YOUR TOASTER OVEN

Roxanne Wyss + Kathy Moore

TILLER PRESS

NEW YORK   LONDON   TORONTO   SYDNEY   NEW DELHI

TILLER PRESS

An Imprint of Simon & Schuster, Inc.
1230 Avenue of the Americas
New York, NY 10020

First Tiller Press trade paperback edition February 2021

TILLER PRESS and colophon are trademarks of Simon & Schuster, Inc.

For information about special discounts for bulk purchases, please contact
Simon & Schuster Special Sales at 1-866-506-1949 or business@simonandschuster.com.

The Simon & Schuster Speakers Bureau can bring authors to your live event.
For more information or to book an event, contact the Simon & Schuster Speakers
Bureau at 1-866-248-3049 or visit our website at www.simonspeakers.com.

Cover and interior design by Matt Ryan
Photography produced by Blueline Creative Group LLC
Visit: www.bluelinecreativegroup.com
Produced by Katherine Cobbs
Photography by Becky Luigart-Stayner
Food Styling by Torie Cox
Prop Styling by Claire Spollen
Food Styling Assistance by Gordon Sawyer
Author photo by Bateman Photography

Manufactured in China

1   3   5   7   9   10   8   6   4   2

Library of Congress Cataloging-in-Publication Data
Names: Wyss, Roxanne, author. | Moore, Kathy, 1952– author.
Title: Toaster oven takeover : easy and delicious recipes to make in your
toaster oven / by Roxanne Wyss and Kathy Moore.
Description: New York : Tiller Press, 2021. | Includes index.
Identifiers: LCCN 2020026529 (print) | LCCN 2020026530 (ebook) | ISBN
9781982157562 (paperback) | ISBN 9781982157579 (ebook)
Subjects: LCSH: Toaster oven cooking. | LCGFT: Cookbooks.
Classification: LCC TX840.T63 W97 2021 (print) | LCC TX840.T63 (ebook) |
DDC 641.5/86—dc23
LC record available at https://lccn.loc.gov/2020026529
LC ebook record available at https://lccn.loc.gov/2020026530

ISBN 978-1-9821-5756-2
ISBN 978-1-9821-5757-9 (ebook)

For everyone who enjoys
sharing a meal with
family + friends.

Contents

Introduction

WHY USE A TOASTER OVEN?

A toaster oven has many uses, yet its compact size reveals that it is truly a kitchen overachiever. Day in and day out you will constantly turn to this superconvenient appliance. Pop a casserole or side dish into the oven. Bake a potato or toast the pecans. Make delicious crostini for an appetizer or toast a bagel for breakfast. Serve just the right size dessert warm from the oven. The list of benefits grows as you use it, since the delicious food you prepare will inspire you to try other toaster oven recipes. Plus, the smart toaster ovens today perform so well that you might forget it is "just" a toaster oven.

A toaster oven offers so many benefits.

No big oven to heat. Your mighty toaster oven preheats more quickly than a regular big oven. What a convenience on a busy evening when you need dinner quickly!

With room enough for a casserole, a roast chicken, a pizza, or to toast several pieces of bread at once, today's toaster ovens are available in a variety of sizes so you can select the one you need.

Use it daily for breakfast, lunch, or dinner. Everyday family meals, as well as servings for one or two, are perfect in the toaster oven. When holidays or feasts come, your trusty toaster oven is ready to handle the overflow and minimize the stress.

Your toaster oven is more energy efficient than the big oven, which makes it a greener choice. Plus, you won't heat up the whole kitchen or strain the air conditioner.

The toaster oven browns food beautifully. The smaller oven means the food is in closer proximity to the heating element, so it often cooks more quickly and creates a delicious crust. Since it is so fast and easy to use, you can use it when toasting nuts, browning a topping on a casserole, melting cheese, and so many other day-in, day-out uses.

Place your toaster oven where you need it. Countertop height means no bending down or lifting heavy dishes. It is the perfect appliance to place by the bar or in the game room so snacks are close by. And since so many homes today feature an outdoor kitchen or enclosed porch, the toaster oven is easy to carry outside when dining or entertaining al fresco.

The even heat of today's toaster oven will allow you to bake photo-ready food for that Instagram post.

Oh yes, and they make your daily toast, but you are not limited to thin slots. Now you can toast your favorite pastry, thick slices of artisan bread, English muffins, or bagels. You will quickly fall in love with warm slices of banana bread, and you can heat a piece of coffee cake in minutes.

Today's toaster oven is a pro in the kitchen. Thanks to electronic controls, a very accurate thermostat, even heating systems, and adjustable cooking racks, the toaster oven of today is a long way from those sold even a few years ago. Your toaster oven may have a Pizza setting, or a Convection Oven setting, or any of a number of other specialty settings. You will still find a setting for toast, bake, and broil, so the basics are there, but electronic controls allow you to easily cook a nearly endless array of delicious foods.

1

BASICS

Be a Toaster Oven Pro— Let's Get Cooking

Place the toaster oven securely on the counter or a table and allow space for air flow all around the appliance. It is awkward to move, so you won't want to move it daily, which is how often you will use the oven. The oven will be hot, so do not touch it while operating.

Many countertop manufacturers recommend to avoid operating hot appliances on granite, quartz, or other countertops. Place the toaster oven on a heatproof board large enough to hold it securely and protect the counter.

Read the use and care booklet that came with your toaster oven. You will uncover a lot of tips and suggestions. Be sure to follow all of the recommendations for safe operation.

Breaking It Down

These are the various elements and functions usually included with your toaster oven.

REMOVABLE RACK

Many toaster ovens offer different heights for the cooking rack. Often you place the rack in the middle position for toasting bread, and the lowest position when baking, but check what the manufacturer of your oven recommends.

CRUMB TRAY

Toaster ovens are equipped with a crumb tray. Wash it frequently and always position it correctly before cooking. No matter how tempting it might be, do not ever line the crumb tray, unless the manufacturer of your particular toaster oven recommends it.

SETTINGS

Electronic settings typically include one for each function—such as toasting, baking, or broiling—a temperature setting, a timer, and an on/off switch.

FUNCTIONS

Today's toaster ovens may have five, ten, or even more different functions. Here are the most common ones.

TOAST: Often the toast setting allows you to choose the number of bread slices and if you prefer lighter or darker browning.

BAKE: This popular setting is one you will use when baking a casserole, a cake, a batch of cookies, or many other foods. Once you select the bake function, set the temperature, just like you would for a big oven. Usually you place the rack in the lowest position when baking and allow the toaster oven to preheat to the desired temperature.

BROIL: Use the broil setting for broiled meats. It is also the ideal function to use when browning a crisp topping on a casserole or browning and crisping wings or ribs. Place the food on a broiler pan and adjust the rack height as needed for the food. While the top rack position may work well for some thinner foods, the center or a lower position may be best when broiling meat or the top of a casserole.

BAGEL: This is a variation of the toast setting and is designed to brown and crisp the top of a bagel while warming the bottom of the bagel, which makes it ideal for bagels, of course, but also for English muffins or any thicker pastry. Be sure to place the bagel with the cut side facing up.

ROAST: Yes, you can roast a chicken or a wide array of vegetables in your toaster oven. It is very similar to using the baking function, but may offer a longer timer setting. When roasting, the food is not covered and develops a beautiful brown crust.

PIZZA: This preset function is an ideal way to bake a pizza.

CONVECTION: A fan circulates the hot air when you set the toaster oven on convection. Many restaurants and commercial bakeries have used convection heat for many years to ensure even browning with crisp crusts. Because it is more efficient, the baking time is often a little less than regular baking. See tips on page 9.

WARM: Does your oven have a Keep Warm setting? It is great to use after cooking, when you need to keep the dish warm for a little while. Do not use this setting for actual cooking or reheating. Just let the hot food stay in the oven, then set the toaster oven to the warm setting. Do not try to keep food warm too long, for it will dry out or begin to overcook. For optimum food safety, the USDA recommends to keep hot foods above 140°F or cold foods below 40°F. Any food that is kept at room temperature for more than two hours should be discarded.

Many toaster ovens now come with several other settings, such as air frying, dehydrating, heating frozen foods, slow cooking, and many more. Read the use and care manual that came with your oven, or visit the manufacturer's website to get accurate, detailed information for the various settings on your toaster oven.

Toaster Oven Pro Tips

Use hot pads and be careful. The toaster oven, racks, pans, and food itself will be hot.

Preheat the oven on the desired setting and temperature. You may not need to preheat when toasting, but preheating will be common for most other uses.

Which Pans Are Safe to Use?

A number of pans will fit in your toaster oven and many stores sell an ever-increasing array. Common pans that typically fit include pie pans, round or square 8- or 9-inch cake pans, 1- or 2-quart casserole dishes, loaf pans, 6-cup muffin pans, and many more.

It is wise to check the fit before you prepare the dish. If purchasing new pans, double-check the dimensions of the pans and the interior of your oven.

Handles on the pans may limit the fit. Baking pans are listed by the interior dimension, so a 9-inch pie pan measures 9 inches across the inside center. If it has decorative handles, the exterior dimension may measure 10 inches or more.

Large pans—especially 9 x 13-inch baking pans, 12-inch pizza pans, or baking sheets, including one commonly called a "quarter sheet pan"—increase the variety of foods you can prepare, but watch their fit. Some toaster ovens will accommodate larger pans and others will not.

Your toaster oven may have come with a two-piece broiler pan. The broiler pan will have two pieces—the rack, or perforated top, and a solid baking pan on the bottom. When broiling, use both pans so the food rests on the perforated top and any grease or drippings collect in the bottom pan. The bottom baking pan fits perfectly in your toaster oven. We often list a 12 x 12-inch baking pan in our recipes, as it fit in the ovens we used for testing these recipes. Yours may measure slightly differently, but the bottom baking pan of that broiler pan set will work beautifully in your oven, and if it is similar in size to the one listed in the recipe, you will find it convenient to use. If it is substantially smaller in size, you may need to cook the food in batches.

For casseroles and one-dish meals, we often turn to deep 11 x 7 x 2½-inch casserole dishes. These baking dishes are deeper than many 11 x 7-inch metal pans and are ideal for casseroles.

If you have a 9 x 5-inch loaf pan, now is the perfect time to get it out and use it. Many foods are ideal for the loaf pan, which typically fits in the toaster oven. A 9 x 5-inch loaf pan holds about 8 cups, so it is easy to substitute this loaf pan for a 2-quart casserole dish.

Never force a pan to fit or wedge it inside the oven. Be sure the pan allows air flow around the edges and allows the door to close correctly. Check that the top of the pan does not rest too closely to the top heating element; if it does, the oven may not heat evenly and the top of the food may overbrown.

What Is That Baking Pan Made Of?

Metal, oven-safe baking pans are a natural choices. If they fit, they are a win!

Ceramic, stoneware, or glass? Even those labeled oven-safe pose a risk. Always doublecheck the label or information that came with the baking dish. If information on the baking pan is not available, check for guidelines on that company's website or call and ask for directions. Many manufacturers of oven-safe, tempered glass, such as Pyrex and Anchor Hocking, do not recommend using their glass baking dishes in a toaster oven. They explain that even though the oven-safe glass is designed for a regular oven, the glass dish may heat unevenly or rest too closely to the heating element in a toaster oven, and this will cause the dish to break or the oven to malfunction.

Ceramic or stoneware dishes that are oven safe can generally be used in a toaster oven on the baking or roasting cycles. Check their labels carefully if you plan to set the toaster oven on broil.

One more tip. A dark-colored pan absorbs heat, so it will increase the browning on the food and create a darker crust. A shiny, light-colored pan will bake foods with a lighter crust.

Aluminum Foil Versus Parchment Paper

Do not put any container made of paper, plastic, or foam in a toaster oven. Remember, a toaster oven is not a microwave oven. Do not line the crumb tray with foil or parchment paper unless the manufacturer of your particular toaster oven recommends it.

We occasionally suggest covering a filled baking pan or lining the bottom of a pan with aluminum foil or parchment paper. Both offer benefits, but both have risks and need to be used carefully and correctly.

ALUMINUM FOIL

Aluminum foil can be safely used to cover a filled baking pan or to line the bottom of a pan so cleanup is easier. Be sure to fold the foil tightly against the pan. Do not allow corners or edges to stand up from the pan.

We often choose nonstick aluminum foil, as you don't have to spray the foil or pan with cooking spray. If you use regular aluminum foil to line a pan, you may find it best to spray the foil with nonstick cooking spray or lightly grease the foil.

Never line the crumb tray, either part of the boiler pan when broiling, the racks, oven bottom, or the oven sides with aluminum foil. Be sure any aluminum foil does not touch the top, bottom, or surfaces in the toaster oven or rest close to the heating element. The foil can cause the oven to overheat, and if grease or oil collects in the crumb tray or broiler pan, the grease can catch fire.

The warranty on some toaster ovens is voided if you use any aluminum foil in the oven. Read carefully and follow those recommendations.

PARCHMENT PAPER

Parchment paper is frequently used to line the bottom of baking pans, and the grease- and moisture-proof paper is ideal for use when baking cookies or other items. To use the paper, line just the bottom of the pan, cutting the paper to fit. Do not allow the corners or edges of the paper to stand up from the pan. Parchment paper will burn easily, and if it comes close to the heating element you will have a fire hazard.

Never use parchment paper to line the crumb tray or oven racks.

Check with the manufacturer of your toaster oven or of your aluminum foil or parchment paper for specific recommendations regarding use in a toaster oven, the maximum temperatures allowed, or other important directions.

Cooking Times

The cooking times listed in the recipes are estimates. We have carefully tested each recipe to give you the best possible flavor and overall results. The exact cooking time will vary with your personal preferences, the brand and design of your toaster oven, the material your baking pan is made of, the temperature of the food as it begins to cook, the size and shape of the food, and many other variables.

Watch the cooking progress carefully, especially the first few times you use your toaster oven. Many toaster ovens bake and brown more quickly than regular ovens. Once you use your toaster oven a few times, you will be better able to predict if you prefer the food cooked using the minimum or maximum cooking times, or if you need to extend the cooking time listed by a minute or two.

For some foods, like a whole chicken or foods that may rest closer to the heating element, you will see that they brown more quickly than they might in a big oven. Check the cooking progress and be sure they are done through.

Check to see if the food is fully cooked when the cooking cycle goes off, but be careful, as the oven, food, pan, and racks will be hot. When possible, we provide a description of what to look for. Should the crust be brown, the edges crisp, the vegetables tender, or what?

The most accurate test to determine if meat is fully cooked is by inserting an instant-read meat thermometer into the center of the meat, not touching any bone or fat. Position the meat thermometer in the thickest portion of a roast or meat loaf, or in the breast or thigh of a whole chicken. (Do not leave a meat thermometer in the food as it cooks, as there isn't enough room in the toaster oven and the thermometer can easily hit the heating element.)

The USDA lists the following minimum temperatures:

- **Steaks, chops, or roasts**—whether they are beef, lamb, or pork—must reach a minimum temperature of 145°F, then rest for at least 3 minutes.

- **Ground meat, including ground beef, pork, lamb, and veal,** should be cooked to a minimum temperature of 160°F.

- **All poultry, including all ground chicken or turkey,** must reach a minimum temperature of 165°F.

- **Fish** should reach a minimum temperature of 145°F.

Once you remove meat from the oven, it should rest for 3 to 5 minutes before serving. The resting time not only allows the temperature to climb, the meat will be juicier if allowed to rest before slicing.

Tips for the Convection Oven Setting

Recipes throughout the book often have a convection oven variation. Not all toaster ovens have a Convection Oven setting, but if yours does, it offers even heat and faster cooking. Convection cooking has been used for many years, especially in commercial bakeries and restaurants, where even browning and faster cooking is a must.

How does it work? If you live in a climate where reporters often mention "wind chill," you know that cold wind will make it feel colder outside. The same is true for hot air, so if hot air circulates over the food, the food will brown more quickly and may bake a little faster.

Foods with crisp crusts—such as biscuits, yeast breads, pies, and pastries, as well as roasted meats and crisp, oven-fried food—are ideal for convection oven baking.

Not all foods benefit from convection oven cooking. A recipe that is baked in a covered pan won't benefit from the swirling hot air of a convection oven. Neither will delicate foods, such as baked eggs or foods that easily dry out.

We list the convection oven alternative on those recipes that especially benefit from the swirling hot air. Check the directions that came with your toaster oven to see if it has that setting, and if so, how it should be used. Some models will offer specific suggestions to alter, or sometimes reduce, the cooking time and temperature.

The food often cooks a little faster on the Convection Oven setting, so we trim a few minutes off the recommended cooking time. However, you may not notice as much of a difference in a toaster oven as you might in a larger oven, since the toaster oven is a small cavity and the food rests more closely to the heating element than it does in a big oven.

In large ovens, the standard is to reduce the oven temperature by 25°F when using the Convection Oven setting. We did not find this to be consistently true in every toaster oven.

Some toaster ovens now come with both a convection setting and an air fryer setting. An air fryer is known for high-velocity air, similar to a convection setting but with more quickly swirling air. When using an air fryer, the food is placed in a basket or on a special rack over a drip pan, which allows the hot air to circulate on all sides of the food, creating a brown, crisp crust. Various brands of toaster ovens perform quite differently, and sometimes the Convection Oven setting and the Air Fry setting seem to perform quite similarily, yet are labeled differently, and other times both settings perform as unique settings, and each performs quite well. Only you will know which is true with your toaster oven.

Experiment a little and see how your toaster oven performs on that setting. Use the convection oven variation listed in the recipe as a starting point to reduce the cooking time. After a few uses you will determine if you like the results better if you lower the temperature 10, 15, or even 25 degrees from that listed in the recipe.

It is best to watch the cooking progress during the last few minutes of the baking time. Even though the food is browned, double-check that it is fully cooked and that the meat thermometer registers the necessary temperature.

Toast

We spent much of our career in a test kitchen for a small appliance company, so we tested many toasters, slice after slice, checking for even browning. The engineers would ask if this toaster model or that brand of thermostat worked better, or which heating elements heated evenly. But none of those tests altered the unbeatable and comforting flavor and aroma of toast. We can offer a few tips:

Various brands and types of bread toast differently. Just because you like a particular setting for thin white bread does not mean you will like that same setting for thick slices of artisan bread. Experiment with the settings for the various breads you toast. Fresh bread may toast differently than slices from an older loaf.

Generally sweeter or buttery bread needs a shorter toasting time than firmer, whole-grain breads.

Place the bread slices directly on the toaster oven rack. Do not place them in a pan. On the other hand, when toasting thin slices of a baguette for crostini or toasting other small breads, it is easier and safer to arrange the slices on a 12 x 12-inch baking pan or pizza pan. Midway through the toasting, turn the slices over to toast the second side. Use a hot pad to lift the pan out of the oven and carefully turn the bread.

The number-one variable is your personal preference, and it is fine if you like a light, golden toast or if you enjoy a darker, crispier crust.

For a simple yet delicious treat, spread some butter on the toast while it's still warm from the toaster oven, then eat it immediately. Or you can follow the lead of trendy restaurants and bakeries, which offer all kinds of specialty bread toasts and toppings. A few of our favorites include avocado toast, a smear of Nutella, peanut butter or other nut butters, such as almond butter, jams, herbed butters, hummus, honey, and so many more. For a brunch or shower, you could create a toast bar with your toaster oven and set out a variety of breads and toppings. Experiment a little and see what you enjoy.

What Can I Cook in My Toaster Oven?

Here is a guide to some common foods that are ideal for your toaster oven.

If baking a frozen or commercially prepared food, follow the package directions. Use the Frozen setting if your toaster oven has one. As a toaster oven can often bake and brown more quickly than a big oven, watch the cooking progress during the last few minutes of baking.

FOOD	SETTING + TEMPERATURE	TIME ESTIMATE	NOTES
Bacon	Bake; 350°F	10 to 15 minutes	Separate the slices and place in a single layer on a baking pan. Bake until crisp, turning the slices midway through the baking time.
Bread crumbs, toasted	Bake; 350°F	10 to 15 minutes	Process the bread in a food processor to form fine crumbs. Toss the crumbs in 1 tablespoon olive oil and season with kosher salt. Spread in a thin layer on a baking sheet and bake until golden brown and toasted.
Burgers	Broil	12 to 13 minutes	Shape into patties about ½ inch thick. Place the burgers on a two-piece broiler pan and adjust the rack so the meat is about 2 to 4 inches from the heat source. Turn the burgers midway through cooking. Check the temperature of the meat with a meat thermometer, and cook ground beef or pork until it registers 160°F. (Ground chicken or turkey to 165°F.)
Cookies	Bake; 350°F	8 to 14 minutes	Follow the recipe or package label. Space the cookies about 2 inches apart on a baking pan. Bake until golden brown.
Crostini	Toast or Bake; 400°F	3 to 5 minutes on Toast or 6 to 10 minutes on Bake	Crostini are crisp slices of toasted baguette, which are perfect for many appetizers. Slice the baguette thinly and arrange the slices on the rack and toast. Or, for an easier and safer method, arrange the bread on a baking pan, and bake until the bread is golden brown and crisp, turning midway through the baking for even browning. For authentic flavor, rub the toast with the cut side of a garlic clove, then brush lightly with extra-virgin olive oil.
Croutons	Bake; 375°F	8 to 10 minutes	Cut your favorite bread into ¼ to ½-inch cubes. Any bread will work, and a rustic artisan bread is especially good. Making croutons is a great use for leftover bread. Toss the bread in 1 to 2 tablespoons of olive oil or melted butter. Season with kosher salt, and if desired, dry minced herbs such as rosemary, thyme, or parsley. For garlic, mince the garlic and add it to the olive oil or melted butter. Bake 5 minutes, stir then bake an additional 3 to 5 minutes or until the cubes are golden brown and toasted. If you wish to add grated Parmesan cheese, sprinkle it over the bread cubes after stirring.
Frozen french fries or potato puffs	Bake; 425°F or per package instructions	20 to 25 minutes	Spread the frozen french fries in a single layer on a baking pan. Bake until crisp and golden brown, stirring midway through the baking time.
Frozen pie	Bake; 425°F or per package instructions	1 hour to 1 hour 15 minutes	Place the frozen pie on a baking sheet and position the rack at the lowest position. Bake according to the package directions, baking until golden brown.

FOOD	SETTING + TEMPERATURE	TIME ESTIMATE	NOTES
Frozen pizza	Bake or Pizza setting; 425°F to 450°F or per package instructions	10 to 15 minutes	Place the pizza on a pizza pan. Follow the package instructions, baking until the pizza is browned and the cheese is melted and bubbly.
Garlic, roasted	Bake; 400°F	20 to 30 minutes	Peel and discard the papery outer skin of the garlic head. Slice the top ¼ inch off the top of the garlic head with a sharp knife. Place the garlic head on sheet of aluminum foil, drizzle with olive oil and season with kosher salt and freshly ground black pepper. Wrap the foil tightly to make a sealed packet and place on a baking sheet. Bake until the garlic is tender. Allow to cool. Note: When making a foil wrap, as when roasting the garlic head, be sure to make the packet compact and place it so it is not near the heating element.
Nuts, toasted	Bake; 350°F	5 to 7 minutes	Spread the nuts in a single layer on a baking pan. Bake until golden brown and toasted.
Potatoes, baked	Bake; 350°F	45 to 55 minutes	Select russet potatoes about 6 to 8 ounces each. Scrub the potatoes, then pierce several times with the tines of a fork. Rub the potato evenly all over with olive oil, canola oil, or vegetable oil. Sprinkle with kosher salt. Place the potatoes on the rack and bake until tender and the skin is crisp.
Reheat leftovers	Bake, 350°F		Reheat food until it is steaming hot (over 165°F), but take care not to overcook or dry out the food. For a casserole or meat, cover the food. Stir or rearrange the food midway through cooking. Pizza, pies, and other foods with crisp crust should not be covered. To reheat pizza by the slice, heat the piece about 5 minutes or until hot. If desired, add a sprinkling of fresh cheese during the last few minutes.
Steak, broiled	Broil		Place the steak on a two-piece broiler pan. Adjust the rack so the meat is about 2 to 4 inches from the heat source. Turn the steak midway through cooking. Check the temperature of the meat with a meat thermometer, cooking to desired doneness. For medium rare, cook until the meat thermometer registers 145°F; for medium cook until 160°F. Times listed are total estimated cooking time: **Rib eye steak 1 inch thick:** 14 to 18 minutes **Sirloin 1 inch thick:** 16 to 21 minutes **Strip steak 1½ inches thick:** 14 to 18 minutes Allow to rest before serving.
Vegetables, roasted	Bake; 425°F	20 to 25 minutes	Cut the vegetables into evenly sized pieces, toss with olive oil, season as desired, and place on a baking pan. Bake, uncovered, for 20 to 25 minutes or until tender as desired, stirring midway through the baking.

Toaster Oven Pantry

MILK

The standard for cooking is whole milk, but we realize that many people today choose low-fat milk. Whole milk will provide the best flavor and texture, but lower fat milk will work, too. These recipes were tested using fresh dairy milk, but other milks such as almond or soy can be substituted, if you prefer.

We love the flavor of buttermilk, but if you don't have buttermilk, pour 1 tablespoon white vinegar or lemon juice into a 1-cup liquid measuring cup and add milk to equal 1 cup. Allow it to stand for a few minutes, then measure out the volume you need for the recipe you are preparing.

We use buttermilk frequently, and always want to keep it handy, so we keep it frozen. This is perfect to do when you have half a carton left and need to use it. Pour the buttermilk into an ice cube tray and freeze it. Once frozen, pop out the buttermilk cubes and seal them in a zip-top freezer bag to store. Thaw the buttermilk you need in the refrigerator in a covered small bowl or jar. Or heat in the microwave on low (10 percent power) in 10-second intervals or until thawed. It will separate, so whisk or shake it to combine before using. For optimum flavor, use frozen buttermilk within about three months.

BUTTER

Unsalted stick butter was used for the recipes in this cookbook. For optimum flavor, we do not recommend margarine. Low-fat, light, soft, whipped, or tub-style butter all have a different formulation than stick butter and are not recommended for these recipes.

Softened butter means a slight indentation remains when the butter is touched lightly, but the butter still holds its shape. You can set the butter out of the refrigerator for about 30 to 60 minutes, depending on the temperature of the kitchen, but don't let the butter sit out for several hours on a hot afternoon. If time is short and you forgot to put it out, you can cut the butter into pieces and place it on a microwave-safe glass plate. Microwave on medium-low (20 percent) power for 10 to 15 seconds for ¼ cup of butter, or for 20 to 25 seconds for ½ cup of butter, then allow it to stand for 10 minutes. Do not melt the butter unless the recipe lists melted butter. You might also grate the cold butter using a box grater and it will soften quickly.

EGGS

Large eggs were used for testing these recipes. Results will not be consistent if you use medium or jumbo eggs or an egg substitute.

FLOUR

All-purpose flour is often used in recipes. You will need to experiment if you substitute gluten-free or other specialty flours. To measure all-purpose flour, spoon the flour out of the canister into a dry measuring cup, and then level it off with the flat edge of a butter knife or spatula. Do not dip the measuring cup into the flour or shake the cup to level it off. Flour does not need to be sifted for the recipes in this book.

SALT

Kosher salt is preferred when cooking savory dishes. There is a big flavor difference between brands, so taste and adjust the seasoning level to suit your personal preferences. We use table salt when baking.

OIL

We typically use olive oil, for the flavor it imparts, or turn to canola or vegetable oil, which is a flavorless "neutral" oil.

Olive oil is very popular due to both its excellent flavor and the added health benefits, but do you know when to use olive oil and when extra-virgin olive oil might be the best choice? Extra-virgin olive oil is considered the finest olive oil and the flavor is excellent, but since it is the most expensive, it is best used in salad dressings when the flavor is obvious. Also, if you use it for frying, the flavor may break down due to the higher temperatures, so the added expense is a waste. Therefore, we recommend using virgin olive oil when you sauté or bake and keep the extra-virgin olive oil for dressings.

NONSTICK COOKING SPRAY

Who likes to clean stuck-on food from the edges and corners of a baking pan? We sure don't, so we often spray baking pans with nonstick cooking spray. If you prefer not to use a nonstick spray, use a little oil or shortening on a paper towel and lightly wipe, or grease, the pan. Some nonstick-coated baking pans caution against using cooking spray, and if you do, it may void the warranty on that pan. Read the user information from the manufacturer of the pan to see if nonstick cooking spray is allowed. Some companies will recommend using only nonstick cooking spray with flour on their pan, so read the label on your nonstick cooking spray to see which you own.

Do not spray the inside of the toaster oven or the crumb tray with nonstick cooking spray.

Selecting a Toaster Oven

Whether you are looking to purchase your first toaster oven or think you might need to upgrade to a newer model, here are several tips that will help you make the best decision.

As with any small appliance, first think about what you might want to cook with it. Reading this cookbook will introduce you to a wide range of foods that are perfectly prepared in your toaster oven. What sounds especially good to you or what would your family enjoy?

How many slices of bread do you want to toast at once? Many ovens are rated by the number of slices of bread, so you might want choose one that toasts four, six, or nine slices of bread at once. What pans do you want to fit into your oven? Are you cooking for one or two, or for several? Do you want it to hold a frozen pizza?

Where do you hope to place the toaster oven? Will it comfortably fit in the allotted space, clearing any cabinet above it and still allow air circulation around it?

How does the door open? Does it open in such a way that you have easy access inside the oven from where you might typically stand?

Does the oven you are considering come with pans or accessories? Does the two-piece broiler pan that comes with the oven feel sturdy and easy to clean? If you want to use a pizza stone, a rotisserie, or an air fryer basket in your toaster oven, now is the time to consider that.

How many racks and rack positions are there? Is the crumb tray easy to remove and return to its correct position, and easy to clean?

Most toaster ovens will toast, bake, and broil. If you know that bagels are a standard breakfast in your house, or you want to heat lots of frozen pizzas, those should be important settings for you. Do you want to dehydrate foods or air fry? Check the list of settings so you can select an oven that will perform as you want it to.

Once you get familiar with the controls, you'll find most are easy to use, but some appear easier than others. Can you turn the Convection setting on or off, or is it set to convection cook all of the time? Is there an interior light? Can you easily set the timer?

What is the wattage? Generally, the higher the wattage, the faster the toaster oven will heat up.

Cleaning

We could list lots of reasons why, but trust us when we say that it is easier to clean the toaster oven after each use. Unplug the toaster oven before cleaning. Follow the manufacturer's directions for specifics, but if you wipe the door and wash the racks and crumb tray after each use, it will stay cleaner. Do not let fat and grease build up or bake on.

2

BREAKFAST
+
BRUNCH

Granola

2 cups old-fashioned oats

2/3 cup sliced almonds or chopped pecans, walnuts, or cashews

1 tablespoon flax seeds

2 teaspoons white sesame seeds

1/2 teaspoon kosher salt

1/2 teaspoon ground cinnamon

3 tablespoons olive oil

3 tablespoons maple syrup

1 1/3 cups dried fruit such as raisins, cherries, or chopped apricots

CONVECTION OVEN VARIATION: Prepare the granola as directed. Bake on the Convection Oven setting at 350°F for 8 minutes, stir, and bake for an additional 5 to 7 minutes, or until the oats are golden brown. Remove from the oven, stir in the dried fruit, and continue as the recipe directs.

If hearing the word *granola* makes you think ho-hum, think again. This recipe can be prepared with pantry items and baked in a matter of minutes. Yogurt parfaits will be transformed to a new level, and if you need an afternoon pick-me-up, granola can be your go-to snack.

1. Preheat the toaster oven to 350°F.

2. Combine the oats, nuts, flax seeds, sesame seeds, salt, and cinnamon in a large bowl. Place the olive oil and maple syrup in a small bowl and stir. Pour the oil-syrup mixture over the oat mixture and stir until coated well.

3. Spread the granola in a 12 x 12-inch baking pan. Bake, uncovered, for 10 minutes. Stir and continue to bake for an additional 6 to 8 minutes, or until the oats are golden brown. Remove from the oven and stir in the dried fruit. Set on a wire rack to cool. Store in a sealed jar or container for up to two weeks.

TIP: Freeze granola for longer storage, up to 6 months.

Pecan-Topped Baked Oatmeal

SERVES 6

This overnight breakfast casserole turns a bowl of oatmeal into something special, yet it still captures all of the warm, comforting flavor you long for in a bowl of oats. It is one of Kathy's favorite breakfast dishes, and she serves it when her family gathers at their annual reunion. It couldn't be easier—just assemble it the night before, refrigerate it, then bake it in the morning.

1. Lightly butter an 8 x 8-inch square baking pan.

2. Melt 2 tablespoons butter; set aside to cool slightly.

3. Whisk the eggs in a large bowl. Add the milk, brown sugar, cinnamon, vanilla, and salt and whisk to combine. Stir in the oats. Stir in the melted butter. Pour into the prepared pan. Cover and refrigerate overnight.

4. When ready to bake, preheat the toaster oven to 350°F. Gently stir the oat mixture in the baking pan.

5. Make the topping: Blend the brown sugar and pecans in a small bowl. Sprinkle the pecan mixture over the top of the oats. Bake, uncovered, for 40 to 45 minutes or until it is set and a knife inserted in the center comes out clean.

6. Sprinkle with fresh blueberries, if desired. Spoon into bowls and serve with milk to drizzle on top.

TIPS: Are you cooking for a small family? Cut the recipe in half and pour into a buttered 9 x 5-inch loaf pan. Bake as directed for 35 to 40 minutes or until it is set and a knife inserted in the center comes out clean.

If you prefer, use your favorite nondairy milk in this recipe.

2 tablespoons unsalted butter, plus additional for the pan

2 large eggs

3 cups whole milk

¼ cup packed dark brown sugar

1 teaspoon ground cinnamon

1 teaspoon pure vanilla extract

¼ teaspoon kosher salt

3 cups old-fashioned oats

TOPPING

¼ cup packed dark brown sugar

½ cup chopped pecans

Fresh blueberries (optional)

Milk (optional)

CONVECTION OVEN VARIATION: Prepare the oatmeal as directed. Bake on the Convection Oven setting at 350°F for 30 to 35 minutes or until it is set and a knife inserted in the center comes out clean. Proceed as the recipe directs.

Italian Strata

1 cup boiling water

3 tablespoons chopped sun-dried tomatoes (dry-packed)

5 cups cubed French bread or country bread (cut into 1-inch cubes)

Nonstick cooking spray

1½ ounces sliced turkey pepperoni, cut into fourths (about ¾ cup)

2 tablespoons chopped pepperoncini peppers

1 cup coarsely chopped fresh spinach

1 cup shredded Italian blend cheese or mozzarella cheese

4 large eggs

1½ cups whole milk

1 teaspoon Italian seasoning

¼ teaspoon kosher salt

2 tablespoons shredded Parmesan cheese

Think of a gourmet version of breakfast pizza that would be perfect for brunch, lunch, or even dinner with friends. It is easy for entertaining because you can make the strata the day before. In the morning, before friends arrive, toss a salad and you can enjoy the gift of time with your friends, family, and loved ones.

1. Pour the boiling water the over sun-dried tomatoes in a small, deep bowl; set aside.

2. Preheat the toaster oven to 350°F. Place the bread cubes on a 12 x 12-inch baking pan. Bake for 10 minutes, stirring once.

3. Spray an 8 x 8-inch square baking pan with nonstick cooking spray. Drain the sun-dried tomatoes and pat dry with paper towels. Arrange half the bread cubes evenly in the prepared pan. Top with half the pepperoni, half the pepperoncini, all the spinach, and all of the reconstituted tomatoes. Sprinkle with ½ cup of the Italian cheese. Repeat layers with the remaining bread, pepperoni, pepperoncini, and ½ cup cheese.

4. Whisk the eggs, milk, Italian seasoning, and salt in a large bowl. Pour the egg mixture over the bread layers. Press down lightly with the back of a large spoon. Sprinkle with the Parmesan cheese. Cover and chill for at least 2 hours or overnight.

5. Preheat the toaster oven to 350°F. Bake the strata, uncovered, for 35 to 45 minutes, or until a knife inserted into the center comes out clean. Let stand for 10 minutes before serving.

Baked Egg Cups

SERVES 2

Toast, ham, and eggs baked in one delicious cup is a great way to start your day. These baked egg cups are quick to assemble, then pop them into the toaster oven and let them bake while you get ready for your day.

1. Preheat the toaster oven to 350°F. Spray 2 (8-ounce) oven-safe ramekins with nonstick cooking spray.

2. Trim the crusts off the bread. (Discard the crusts or save for another use.) Lightly spread one side of each slice of bread with butter. Gently press the bread down into the ramekins, butter-side up, shaping to fit. Trim the ham slices so they fit the cup and arrange the strips of ham evenly over the bread. (The ham strips should not overhang the edges of the cup.) Spoon the cheese evenly over the ham. Add the egg to each cup and season with salt and pepper. Drizzle 1 teaspoon milk over the top of the egg yolk in each cup.

3. Bake, uncovered, for 20 to 25 minutes or until the yolk is lightly set. Remove from the oven and let stand for 2 to 3 minutes. (The residual heat will continue to cook the egg yolk.) Top, as desired, with any of the various topping choices.

TIPS: The milk is drizzled over the yolk before cooking so the yolk does not dry while baking.

Customize your egg cups as you desire. Omit the bread, or substitute crisp cooked bacon strips, cut in thirds so they fit the cup, for the ham.

Nonstick cooking spray

2 slices white or wheat bread

1½ teaspoons unsalted butter, softened

2 thin slices ham, cut into strips about ½ inch wide

2 to 3 tablespoons shredded Swiss or cheddar cheese

2 large eggs

Kosher salt and freshly ground black pepper

2 teaspoons whole milk or half-and-half

Optional toppings: minced fresh flat-leaf (Italian) parsley, basil, tarragon, or other fresh herb, chopped tomatoes, chopped avocado, green onion (white and green parts, thinly sliced)

Freezer-Ready Breakast Burritos

MAKES 8

8 large eggs

2 tablespoons whole milk

Kosher salt and freshly
  ground black pepper

1 tablespoon unsalted butter

1 pound bulk breakfast
  sausage

1 medium russet potato,
  peeled and finely chopped

2 green onions, white and
  green portions, chopped

8 flour tortillas, about
  8 inches in diameter

1 cup shredded sharp cheddar
  cheese

Salsa

Optional toppings:
  guacamole, chopped
  avocado, chopped tomato

Make a batch of these breakfast burritos and stash them, ready to bake, in the freezer. Set those you want to serve in the refrigerator to thaw overnight. Then bake while you get ready for the day and breakfast will be stress-free, and still hot and delicious.

1. Whisk the eggs and milk in a large bowl and season with salt and pepper. Melt the butter in a large skillet over medium heat. Add the eggs and cook, stirring occasionally, until the eggs are softly set. Spoon the cooked eggs into a medium bowl; set aside.

2. Cook the sausage in the same skillet over medium heat until lightly browned, stirring to crumble. Add the potato and cook, stirring frequently, until the sausage is fully cooked and the potato is tender. Stir in the green onions and cook for 2 minutes. Drain.

3. Wrap the tortillas in a clean towel and microwave on High (100 percent power) for 90 seconds or until warm.

4. Spoon the sausage-vegetable mixture, eggs, and cheese evenly into each tortilla. Fold in the sides of the tortilla, then roll gently to form a burrito. Wrap each burrito in aluminum foil, then seal in a freezer bag or container. Label and freeze for up to 1 month.

5. The night before serving, place the number of wrapped burritos you wish to serve in the refrigerator to partially thaw.

6. Preheat the toaster oven to 375°F. Place the foil-wrapped burrito on the rack in the toaster oven. Bake for 20 to 25 minutes or until heated through. Carefully unwrap the burrito and place on a plate. Top with salsa and any of the suggested toppings.

TIP: Substitute $2/3$ cup refrigerated or frozen and thawed hash brown potatoes for the chopped potato.

English Muffin Express Sandwich

Breakfast on the run never tasted so good. You won't be tempted to buy a mediocre breakfast sandwich at a fast food restaurant when you can make one fresh and hot in your toaster oven. And unlike the shop that only sells egg sandwiches in the morning, you can make this anytime.

1. Stir the mayonnaise, green onions, and garlic powder in a small bowl; set aside.

2. Melt 1 tablespoon butter in a small, nonstick skillet over medium heat. Whisk 1 egg in a small bowl and season with salt and pepper. Pour the egg into the skillet. Cook about 1 minute or until the egg is cooked on the bottom, gently turn the egg, and cook the second side. Remove the cooked egg from the skillet and keep warm. Repeat with the second egg.

3. Toast the English muffins in the toaster oven. Remove the toasted muffins and lightly spread the softened butter on the cut surface of each muffin. Place a slice of Canadian bacon and cheese on the bottompiece of each muffin. (Fold the cheese as necessary and do not allow the edges of the cheese to hang over the edges of the muffin.) Place the muffin, cheese-side up, in a baking pan. Heat on Toast or Broil for 1 to 2 minutes or until the cheese is melted.

4. Spread the top piece of each English muffin with the mayonnaise mixture.

5. Remove the cheese-topped English muffin from the toaster oven. Place the cooked egg on top of the melted cheese, folding to fit, as necessary. Top with the other piece of the English muffin, mayonnaise side down. Serve warm.

TIP: Add your favorite toppings, such as sliced tomatoes, sliced avocado, or minced fresh herbs, to your breakfast sandwich.

1 tablespoon mayonnaise

1 tablespoon chopped green onions, white and green portions

¼ teaspoon garlic powder

1 tablespoon unsalted butter, plus softened butter for spreading

2 large eggs

Kosher salt and freshly ground black pepper

2 English muffins, split

2 slices Canadian bacon or thin, deli-style cooked ham

2 slices cheddar cheese

Maple Bacon

12 slices bacon

½ cup packed dark brown sugar

2 tablespoons maple syrup

1 teaspoon Dijon mustard

2 tablespoons red or white wine

CONVECTION OVEN VARIATION: Prepare the recipe as directed. Bake the bacon on the Convection Oven setting at 350°F for 8 minutes or until the bacon is almost crisp. Proceed as the recipe directs, glazing the bacon. Bake for 6 minutes, turn, and brush with the glaze. Bake for an additional 3 to 5 minutes or until golden brown.

This recipe is best done in two batches, but the most important point to remember is to line your pan with foil for easy cleanup. Of course, this is decadent with breakfast or brunch, but I will wager you will find yourself preparing this for a snack.

1. Preheat the oven to 350°F. Line a 12 x 12-inch baking pan with aluminum foil.

2. Place 6 bacon strips on the prepared pan, leaving space between the strips. Bake for 10 minutes or until the bacon is almost crisp. Carefully drain the bacon and return it to the pan.

3. Combine the brown sugar, maple syrup, mustard, and wine in a small bowl. Blend until smooth. Brush the glaze over the bacon. Bake for 8 minutes. Turn the bacon and brush with the glaze. Continue to bake for an additional 6 to 8 minutes, or until golden brown.

4. Repeat with the remaining bacon strips.

Baked French Toast with Maple Bourbon Syrup

SERVES 6

Brunch with friends and family is a special occasion, and this delicious recipe helps to make the event memorable. Best of all, quickly assemble it the evening before, then just bake it in the morning.

1. Spray an 11 x 7 x 2½-inch baking dish with nonstick cooking spray. Pour the butter into the dish. Stir in the brown sugar and pecans. Arrange the bread at an angle in the dish, overlapping the bottom of the slices as necessary.

2. Whisk the eggs, milk, and vanilla in a medium bowl. Drizzle the milk mixture over the bread, taking care to pour slowly and moisten the edges of the bread. Cover and refrigerate overnight.

3. When ready to bake, preheat the toaster oven to 350°F. Bake, uncovered, for 30 to 35 minutes or until golden and set.

4. Mix the maple syrup and bourbon in a small bowl. Drizzle the syrup over the French toast. Bake for 3 to 5 minutes. Let stand for 2 to 3 minutes, then serve warm.

TIP: The alcohol bakes off but leaves a faint but delicious and distinctive flavor. Omit the bourbon if you prefer.

Nonstick cooking spray

4 tablespoons unsalted butter, melted

½ cup packed dark brown sugar

⅔ cup chopped pecans, toasted

6 (1-inch-thick) slices crusty artisan, brioche, or firm country bread

3 large eggs

1 cup milk

1 teaspoon pure vanilla extract

⅓ cup maple syrup

2 tablespoons bourbon

CONVECTION OVEN VARIATION: Prepare the recipe as directed. Bake on the Convection Oven setting at 350°F for 25 to 30 minutes. Prepare the syrup and drizzle over the French toast. Bake for 2 to 3 minutes. Let stand for 2 to 3 minutes, then serve warm.

Apricot Coffee Cake

MAKES 1 COFFEE CAKE

2 cups baking mix

3 ounces cream cheese

¼ cup unsalted butter

½ cup chopped pecans, toasted

⅓ cup whole milk

¾ cup apricot preserves

GLAZE

1 cup confectioners' sugar

¼ teaspoon almond extract

1 to 2 tablespoons whole milk

CONVECTION OVEN VARIATION: Prepare the coffee cake as directed. Bake on the Convection Oven setting at 425°F for 13 to 14 minutes or until golden brown. Glaze the coffee cake as directed.

This recipe is adapted from one Roxanne received from a true Southern gentleman. Quinton A. Wright lived to just shy of celebrating his hundredth birthday. He went by "Q" or "Papa Q," but no matter, he was a master in all things cooking. Spending hours upon hours baking and sharing his love through his baked delicacies was his trademark. He left quite a legacy, and this recipe shall always be a reminder of a man who enjoyed a life well lived.

1. Preheat the toaster oven to 425°F. Grease a 12 x 12-inch baking pan.

2. Place the baking mix in a large bowl. Using a pastry cutter or two knives, cut the cream cheese and butter into the baking mix until the mixture is crumbly throughout. Add the pecans and milk and mix well.

3. Turn the dough onto a lightly floured surface and knead lightly about 8 times. Roll the dough into a 12 x 8-inch rectangle. Place the rolled dough diagonally on the prepared pan. Spread the preserves lengthwise down the center of the dough. Make 2½-inch cuts at 1-inch intervals on both sides of the filling. Fold the strips over the preserves, overlapping in the center. Bake for 15 minutes or until golden brown.

4. Make the Glaze: Whisk the confectioners' sugar, almond extract, and 1 tablespoon milk in a small bowl until smooth. Add additional milk, as needed, to make a glaze consistency.

5. Drizzle the glaze over the warm coffee cake.

TIPS: You can substitute your favorite flavor of preserve, but we especially enjoy apricot. If the preserves are thick and cold, place them in a small glass microwave-safe bowl and heat in the microwave oven on High (100 percent) power for 15 seconds or until just warm.

To make rolling the rectangle easier, form the dough into a 12-inch log and then, using a rolling pin, roll until you have 8 inches across.

PIZZA
+
FLATBREADS

Avocado Chicken Flatbread

SERVES 4

1 tablespoon olive oil

1 clove garlic, minced

1 small avocado, pitted, peeled, and thinly sliced

1 teaspoon fresh lime juice

¼ cup ranch salad dressing

1 tablespoon Sriracha or hot sauce

1 package (10.6 ounces) flatbread pizza crust

¾ cup chopped, cooked chicken

2 slices bacon, cooked until crisp and crumbled

¼ cup chopped red onion

¾ cup shredded Monterey Jack cheese

1 cup thinly sliced romaine or iceberg lettuce

½ cup cherry tomatoes, halved

CONVECTION OVEN VARIATION: Prepare the recipe as directed. Bake the flatbread on the Convection Oven setting at 400°F for 2 to 3 minutes, or until the crust is hot and lightly toasted. Top the crust with the chicken, bacon, onion, and cheese. Bake for 3 to 4 minutes or until the cheese is melted. Proceed as the recipe directs.

Start with a premade flatbread, pizza crust, or naan, then top it with fresh favorites. The ranch dressing takes on a zesty flavor when blended with hot sauce. Be sure to assemble all of the ingredients before starting to toast the crust so you can top the hot crust quickly.

1. Preheat the toaster oven to 400°F.

2. Mix the olive oil and garlic in a small bowl; set aside.

3. Place the avocado slices in a small bowl and drizzle with the lime juice; set aside.

4. Stir the salad dressing and Sriracha in a small bowl; set aside.

5. Brush the garlic olive oil over the flatbread. Place it on a 12-inch pan and bake for 3 to 4 minutes, or until the crust is hot and lightly toasted.

6. Top the crust with the chicken, bacon, onion, and cheese. Bake for 5 minutes or until the cheese is melted. Top with the lettuce, tomatoes, and avocado slices. Drizzle with the ranch dressing mixture.

TIP: Substitute 1 package (8.8 ounces) of naan, with 2 crusts, for the larger flatbread. Prepare one crust, with half of the toppings, as directed, then repeat with the remaining crust and toppings.

French Bread Pizza

SERVES 6

No need to think twice about how to make a pizza crust. This is the ideal recipe to use when you crave a great pizza flavor but want a no-fuss recipe. Just cut the loaf of bread in half and you are on your way. The garlic butter spread adds a delicious depth of flavor to this pizza.

1. Preheat the toaster oven to 450°F.

2. Stir the melted butter, garlic, and Italian seasoning in a small bowl; set aside.

3. Heat the oil in a small skillet over medium-high heat. Add the onion and green pepper and sauté, stirring frequently, for 3 minutes. Add the mushrooms and cook, stirring frequently, for 7 to 10 minutes or until the liquid has evaporated. Remove from the heat; set aside.

4. Gently pull a little of the soft bread out of the center of the loaf, making a well. (Take care not to tear the crust.) Brush the garlic butter over the cut sides of the bread.

5. Place both halves of the bread, side by side, cut side up, on a 12 x 12-inch baking pan. Bake for 3 minutes or until heated through. Carefully remove the bread from the oven.

6. Spoon the pizza sauce evenly over the cut sides of the bread. Top evenly with the Canadian bacon, the onion-mushroom mixture, and the olives. Top with the mozzarella and Parmesan cheeses. Return to the oven and bake for 3 to 5 minutes or until the cheese is melted.

7. Cut the French bread pizza crosswise into slices.

TIPS: Substitute any of your favorite pizza toppings for those listed. Cook the vegetables or meat before placing them on your pizza.

This is an ideal time to use the Pizza setting if your oven has this function. If it has an added Frozen function, leave it off. Bake as directed until the crust is hot and toasted. Top the pizza and bake until the cheese is hot and bubbly.

2 tablespoons unsalted butter, melted

2 cloves garlic, minced

½ teaspoon Italian seasoning

1 tablespoon olive oil

½ cup chopped onion

½ cup chopped green pepper

1 cup sliced button or white mushrooms

1 (10- to 12-ounce) loaf French or Italian bread, about 12 inches long, split in half lengthwise

½ cup pizza sauce

6 to 8 slices Canadian bacon or ¼ cup pepperoni slices

¼ cup sliced ripe olives, drained

1 cup shredded mozzarella cheese

3 tablespoons shredded Parmesan cheese

CONVECTION OVEN VARIATION: Prepare the recipe as directed. Bake the bread on the Convection Oven setting at 450°F for 2 to 3 minutes or until the bread is hot and lightly toasted. Top the bread as directed and bake for 2 to 4 minutes or until the cheese is melted.

Thai Chicken Pizza with Cauliflower Crust

MAKES 1 (11-INCH) PIZZA

Don't feel like you have to give up pizza if you are limiting carbs or gluten. This pizza crust has just the right flavor. Top it with chicken and Thai peanut sauce for a restaurant-style pizza.

1. Preheat the toaster oven to 425°F. Line a 12-inch pizza pan with parchment paper. Spray with nonstick cooking spray.

2. Place the cauliflower in the work bowl of a food processor. Pulse until finely chopped. (Work in batches, as necessary, so as not to overload the food processor.) Transfer the cauliflower rice to a large, microwave-safe bowl. Add 1 tablespoon water. Cover and microwave on High (100 percent) power for 3 minutes or until the cauliflower is tender. Uncover and let the cauliflower cool to room temperature.

3. Spoon the cauliflower into a clean kitchen towel and twist to drain the cauliflower well. Return the drained cauliflower to the bowl. Stir in the eggs, mozzarella, Parmesan, Italian seasoning, and garlic powder and season with salt and pepper. Stir well.

4. Spoon the cauliflower mixture onto the prepared pan. Gently spread or pat the mixture into an even circle, about 11 inches in diameter. Bake for 12 to 15 minutes or until the crust is set and beginning to brown.

5. Meanwhile, make the sauce: Stir the peanut butter, soy sauce, lime juice, honey, vinegar, and chili garlic sauce in a small bowl.

6. Remove the cauliflower crust from the toaster oven. Spread the peanut sauce over the crust. Top with the chicken, carrot, green onions, and Monterey Jack cheese. Bake for 5 minutes or until hot and the cheese is melted.

TIPS: For this recipe, the finely chopped, processed cauliflower measures about 4½ cups. If desired, substitute packaged fresh or frozen riced cauliflower, cook in the microwave oven as directed, then proceed with the recipe.

If you prefer a classic pizza, substitute pizza sauce and your favorite toppings for those listed. Prepare the crust as directed, then top with sauce, cooked vegetables or meat, and cheese as desired. Bake for 5 minutes or until the topping is hot and the cheese is melted.

This also makes a great pizza on a traditional wheat crust. Select your favorite pizza crust recipe or purchase flatbread or naan. Top the crust with the peanut sauce and toppings, then bake until the crust is crisp, the toppings are hot, and the cheese is melted.

Nonstick cooking spray

½ large head cauliflower (about 1 pound), cut into florets (3½ to 4 cups)

2 large eggs, lightly beaten

⅓ cup shredded mozzarella cheese

3 tablespoons shredded Parmesan cheese

2 teaspoons Italian seasoning

½ teaspoon garlic powder

Kosher salt and freshly ground black pepper

SAUCE

¼ cup creamy peanut butter

1½ tablespoons reduced-sodium soy sauce

1½ tablespoons fresh lime juice

1 tablespoon honey

1 tablespoon unseasoned rice vinegar

½ teaspoon chili garlic sauce

TOPPINGS

1 cup chopped or shredded cooked chicken

1 carrot, shredded

2 green onions, white and green portions, thinly sliced

1 cup shredded Monterey Jack cheese

Stromboli

CRUST

2 cups all-purpose flour

2 tablespoons unsalted butter, cut into small pieces

1 teaspoon table salt

2 teaspoons active dry yeast

2 teaspoons sugar

TOPPINGS

½ cup marinara or pizza sauce

½ teaspoon Italian seasoning

2 ounces pepperoni slices

2 ounces salami slices

2 ounces thin ham slices

1½ cups shredded mozzarella cheese

3 tablespoons shredded Parmesan cheese

1 large egg

½ teaspoon granulated garlic

1 teaspoon sesame seeds

CONVECTION OVEN VARIATION: Prepare the recipe as directed. Bake on the Convection Oven setting at 375°F for 22 to 25 minutes or until golden brown.

It is hard to beat the flavor of cheese, meat, and sauce tightly rolled up in a blanket of thin, tender dough. You can always add your favorites to the filling, such as finely chopped vegetables or fresh basil.

1. Make the crust: Place the flour in a large bowl and create a well. Place ⅔ cup water, the butter, and salt in a small microwave-safe bowl and microwave on High (100 percent) power for 30 seconds or until warm. (The temperature of the mixture should not be above 110°F.) Pour the liquid into the well. Sprinkle the yeast and sugar over the water mixture and allow to stand for 5 minutes. Mix the flour mixture until a dough forms. Oil a medium bowl and place the dough in the bowl. Cover and let rise for 1 hour.

2. Preheat the toaster oven to 375°F. Line a 12 x 12-inch baking pan with parchment paper.

3. Flour a clean surface and roll the dough into a 15 x 13½-inch rectangle. Place the dough diagonally on the prepared pan. Spread the marinara sauce over the surface of the dough to within ½ inch of all four edges. Sprinkle with the Italian seasoning. Layer the pepperoni, salami, and ham slices on top of the marinara. Sprinkle with the cheeses. Roll up as tightly as possible and pinch the seams to make sure nothings seeps out.

4. Whisk the egg, 1 tablespoon of water, and the garlic in a small bowl. Brush the egg wash over the stromboli and sprinkle with the sesame seeds. Bake for 25 to 30 minutes or until golden brown.

Family Favorite Pizza

MAKES 1 (11½-INCH) PIZZA

CRUST

½ cup warm water (about 110°F)

1 teaspoon active dry yeast

1½ cups all-purpose flour, plus more for kneading

1 teaspoon kosher salt

½ teaspoon olive oil

TOPPINGS

Pizza sauce

2 cups shredded Italian blend cheese or mozzarella cheese

¼ cup grated Parmesan cheese

Optional toppings: pepperoni slices, cooked crumbled or sliced sausage, vegetables, or other favorite pizza toppings

CONVECTION OVEN VARIATION: Prepare the recipe as directed. Bake the pizza on the Convection Oven setting at 450°F for 16 to 18 minutes, or until the crust is golden brown and the cheese is melted.

No need to wait for pizza dough to rise for an hour with this easy pizza crust. Customize the pizza to your own liking by adding your favorite toppings and cheese.

1. Make the Crust: Pour the water into a medium bowl and sprinkle with the yeast. Let stand for 5 minutes until the yeast is foamy. Add the flour, salt, and olive oil. Mix until a dough forms. Turn the dough out on a floured surface and knead until a ball forms that springs back when you poke a finger into it, about 5 minutes. If the dough is too sticky, add a tablespoon of flour and knead into the dough. Cover the dough and allow to rest for 10 minutes.

2. Preheat the toaster oven to 450°F. Place a 12-inch pizza pan in the toaster oven while it is preheating.

3. Stretch and roll the dough into an 11½-inch round. If the dough starts to shrink back, let it rest for 5 to 10 more minutes and then continue to roll. Carefully remove the hot pan from the toaster oven and place the pizza crust on the hot pan. Top with the desired amount of sauce. Layer cheese and any of your favorite pizza toppings over the pizza.

4. Bake for 18 to 22 minutes, or until the crust is golden brown and the cheese is melted. Let stand for 5 minutes before cutting.

TIP: This is an ideal time to use the Pizza setting if your oven has this function. If it has an added Frozen function, leave it off. Prepare the pizza and bake as directed until the crust is golden brown and the cheese is melted.

Parmesan Artichoke Pizza

MAKES 1 (11½-INCH) PIZZA

Ready for a change from that favorite red-sauce pizza? This artichoke pizza may be the answer. With or without the chicken or the lemon-dressed arugula, it is ideal for dinner, a late-night snack, or even cut into small pieces as an appetizer.

1. Make the Crust: Place the warm water, yeast, and sugar in a large mixing bowl for a stand mixer. Stir, then let stand for 3 to 5 minutes or until bubbly.

2. Stir in the olive oil, salt, whole wheat flour, and 1½ cups bread flour. If the dough is too sticky, stir in an additional 1 to 2 tablespoons bread flour. Beat with the flat (paddle) beater at medium-speed for 5 minutes (or knead by hand for 5 to 7 minutes or until the dough is smooth and elastic). Place in a greased large bowl, turn the dough over, cover with a clean towel, and let stand for 30 to 45 minutes, or until starting to rise.

3. Stir the olive oil, Italian seasoning, and garlic in a small bowl; set aside.

4. Preheat the toaster oven to 450°F. Place a 12-inch pizza pan in the toaster oven while it is preheating.

5. Turn the dough onto a lightly floured surface and pull or roll the dough to make a 12-inch circle. Carefully transfer the crust to the hot pan.

6. Brush the olive oil mixture over the crust. Spread the ricotta evenly over the crust. Top with the artichokes, red onions, fresh basil, Parmesan, and mozzarella. Bake for 13 to 15 minutes, or until the crust is golden brown and the cheese is melted. Let stand for 5 minutes before cutting.

TIPS: If desired, add ¾ cup chopped cooked chicken to the pizza along with the artichokes and red onions.

This is an ideal time to use the Pizza setting if your oven has this function. If it has an added Frozen function, leave it off. Prepare the pizza and bake as directed until the crust is golden brown and the cheese is melted.

VARIATION: Follow the lead of many restaurants and serve fresh greens on the pizza. Whisk 1 tablespoon fresh lemon juice with 1 tablespoon olive oil in a small bowl. Whisk in salt and pepper to taste. Toss 3 cups fresh arugula or spring greens with the lemon juice vinaigrette. Top the pizza with the dressed greens just before serving. Garnish with coarsely shredded Parmesan cheese.

CRUST

¾ cup warm water (110°F)

1½ teaspoons active dry yeast

¼ teaspoon sugar

1 tablespoon olive oil

1 teaspoon table salt

⅓ cup whole wheat flour

1½ to 1⅔ cups bread flour

TOPPINGS

2 tablespoons olive oil

1 teaspoon Italian seasoning

1 clove garlic, minced

½ cup whole milk ricotta cheese, at room temperature

⅔ cup drained, chopped marinated artichokes

¼ cup chopped red onion

3 tablespoons minced fresh basil

½ cup shredded Parmesan cheese

⅓ cup shredded mozzarella cheese

CONVECTION OVEN VARIATION: Prepare the recipe as directed. Bake the pizza on the Convection Oven setting at 450°F for 10 to 15 minutes, or until the crust is golden brown and the cheese is melted.

TOASTS, CROSTINI, + SANDWICHES

Berry Breakfast Bruschetta

SERVES 2

If someone mentions bruschetta you might think of that popular appetizer of garlic toast topped with chopped fresh tomatoes. Now instead of the classic version, imagine toast topped with creamy goat cheese and fresh strawberries. It is the ideal quick breakfast and would be equally tasty as a part of your next brunch menu or as an afternoon snack.

1. Stir the goat cheese and honey in a small bowl. Season generously with pepper. Sprinkle lightly with salt and blend well; set aside.

2. Stir the chopped berries and jam in a small bowl; set aside.

3. Toast the bread in the toaster oven. Spread the goat cheese mixture evenly over the top of each piece of toast. Top each with the fresh berry mixture and sprinkle with the fresh herbs.

TIPS: Substitute any type of berries you prefer or have on hand. Blueberries or raspberries are great choices, or mix and match. Match or complement the type of berry to the jam.

If the jam is thick and cold, place it in a small glass microwave-safe bowl and heat in the microwave oven on High (100 percent) power for 15 seconds or until just warm.

Soft, creamy goat cheese is readily available in a log. Set it at room temperature to soften, then measure by packing it into a measuring cup. If you want to substitute goat cheese crumbles, pour ¼ cup of the crumbles into a small bowl and mash with 1 tablespoon of milk or cream until it is creamy. Proceed as the recipe directs.

¼ cup soft, creamy goat cheese or cream cheese, softened

1 teaspoon honey

Freshly ground black pepper

Dash kosher salt

⅔ cup chopped fresh strawberries

2 teaspoons strawberry jam

2 slices whole grain bread

Fresh basil leaves, thinly sliced, or minced fresh thyme leaves

Goat Cheese Rosemary Crostini with Roasted Garlic + Tomatoes

4 to 5 large cloves garlic, trimmed, not peeled

1½ tablespoons olive oil

2 cups grape tomatoes

Kosher salt and freshly ground black pepper

1 teaspoon balsamic or red wine vinegar

4 ounces soft, creamy goat cheese, softened (about ½ cup)

1 tablespoon minced fresh rosemary leaves

1 baguette loaf, cut into ½-inch-thick slices

Fresh rosemary leaves or minced flat-leaf (Italian) parsley, for garnish (optional)

TIPS: The roasted garlic and tomato mixture is wonderful on the crostini, but we also like it served on grilled chicken, steaks, or chops.

Soft, creamy goat cheese is readily available in a log, and 4 ounces will be about ½ cup of cheese. If you want to substitute goat cheese crumbles, pour ½ cup of the crumbles into a small bowl and mash with 2 tablespoons of milk or cream until it is creamy. Proceed as the recipe directs.

Roasted garlic and tomatoes are fresh and flavorful and make a delicious topping for these crostini. They look beautiful, and the fresh tomato flavor complements the goat cheese and rosemary perfectly.

1. Preheat the toaster oven to 400°F.

2. Place the garlic on an 8- to 12-inch square of aluminum foil and bring up the edges to make a shallow bowl. Drizzle the garlic with ½ tablespoon olive oil. Bring the foil over the garlic and fold the edges to make a sealed packet. Place the packet on one side of a 12 x 12-inch baking pan. (Note: Be sure to make the aluminum foil packet compact and place it on the pan but positioned so it is not near the heating element.)

3. Place the tomatoes in a medium bowl. Drizzle with the remaining tablespoon of olive oil and season with salt and pepper. Pour the tomatoes into a single layer on the other end of the baking pan. Roast, uncovered, for 20 to 25 minutes or until the edges of the tomatoes begin to brown and they are tender.

4. Remove the tomatoes and garlic from the oven and let cool slightly. Spoon the roasted tomatoes, with any collected liquid, into a medium bowl. When the garlic is cool enough to handle, gently squeeze the garlic into a small bowl and discard the garlic peels. Use the back of a spoon to mash the garlic. Stir the roasted garlic and vinegar into the tomatoes. Season with salt and pepper; set aside.

5. Stir the goat cheese and rosemary in a small bowl. Season it generously with pepper. Blend until smooth; set aside.

6. Toast the slices of the baguette in the toaster oven.

7. Distribute the goat cheese mixture evenly over the toasted bread slices. Top with a teaspoon of the roasted tomato-garlic mixture. If desired, garnish with fresh rosemary.

Creamy Bacon + Almond Crostini

MAKES ABOUT 25

1 baguette loaf, cut into ½-inch-thick slices

2 tablespoons olive oil

4 ounces cream cheese, cut into cubes, softened

½ cup mayonnaise

1 cup shredded fontina cheese or Monterey Jack cheese

4 slices bacon, cooked until crisp and crumbled

1 green onion, white and green portions, finely chopped

¼ teaspoon Sriracha or hot sauce

Dash kosher salt

¼ cup sliced almonds, toasted

Minced fresh flat-leaf (Italian) parsley

CONVECTION OVEN VARIATION: Prepare the recipe as directed. Bake the crostini on the Convection Oven setting at 375°F for 5 to 7 minutes, or until the cheese is hot and beginning to melt.

Creamy goodness is the ideal description of these appetizers. Kathy hosts a wine party each year during the holidays, and a batch or two of these crostini are always on the appetizer table.

1. Toast the slices of the baguette in the toaster oven.

2. Arrange the toasted baguette slices on a 12-inch pizza pan or a 12 x 12-inch baking pan. Lightly brush the slices with the olive oil.

3. Preheat the toaster oven to 375°F.

4. Beat the cream cheese and mayonnaise in a medium bowl with an electric mixer at medium speed until creamy and smooth. Stir in the fontina, bacon, green onion, Sriracha, and salt and blend until combined.

5. Distribute the cheese mixture evenly over the toasted bread. Top with the sliced almonds. Bake for 6 to 8 minutes or until the cheese is hot and beginning to melt. Allow to cool for 1 to 2 minutes, then garnish with minced parsley. Serve warm.

TIP: We find that when toasting slices of baguette for crostini, it is easier and safer to arrange the slices on a 12 x 12-inch baking pan or pizza pan instead of placing the slices directly on the oven rack. Midway through the toasting, turn the slices over to toast the second side. Use a hot pad to lift the pan out of the oven and carefully turn the bread.

Mushroom Blue Cheese Crostini

MAKES ABOUT 10 OR 12

You can substitute provolone, Gruyère, or Swiss cheese for the fontina and goat cheese for the blue cheese if you prefer. Either way, pour a glass of wine and enjoy this herby, earthy crostini.

1. Heat the olive oil in a medium nonstick skillet over medium-high heat. Add the mushrooms and cook, stirring frequently, until the liquid has evaporated, 7 to 10 minutes. Add the garlic and cook for 1 minute. Remove from the heat. Stir in the parsley and thyme and season with salt and pepper. Allow the mixture to cool.

2. Toast the slices of bread in the toaster oven.

3. Stir the fontina and blue cheese into the mushroom mixture.

4. Preheat the toaster oven on Broil. Arrange the toasted baguette slices on a 12 x 12-inch baking sheet. Distribute the mushroom cheese mixture evenly over the toasted bread slices. Broil until the cheese melts, 2 to 3 minutes. Drizzle with the lemon juice. Garnish each crostini with a parsley leaf. Serve immediately.

TIP: If using country or artisan bread for this recipe, you may want to slice the pieces into halves or thirds to make a nice-size appetizer.

1 tablespoon olive oil

8 ounces mushrooms, wild or button, sliced

3 cloves garlic, minced

2 tablespoons fresh flat-leaf (Italian) parsley, minced

2 teaspoons chopped fresh thyme, rosemary, or sage leaves

Kosher salt and freshly ground black pepper

10 to 12 country bread, artisan bread, or baguette slices

1 cup grated fontina cheese

½ cup blue cheese or Gorgonzola crumbles

1 tablespoon fresh lemon juice

Whole flat-leaf (Italian) parsley, for garnish

French Vegetable Tartines

SERVES 4

½ medium red bell pepper, cut into ½-inch slices

½ medium red onion, cut into ½-inch slices

2 tablespoons olive oil

Kosher salt and freshly ground black pepper

¾ cup thick-sliced button or white mushrooms

8 asparagus spears, trimmed and halved crosswise

2 tablespoons unsalted butter, softened

1 small clove garlic, minced

1 tablespoon minced fresh rosemary leaves

4 thick slices French or artisan bread

⅓ cup shredded fontina, Gruyère, or Swiss cheese

Minced fresh flat-leaf (Italian) parsley or thyme leaves

CONVECTION OVEN VARIATION: Prepare the recipe as directed. Bake the red pepper and red onion on the Convection Oven setting at 375°F for 8 minutes. Add the asparagus and mushrooms and bake for 5 to 7 minutes, or until the vegetables are tender. Proceed as the recipe directs.

Any day you can instantly feel as if you are sitting at a little table in front of a French café is a good one. A French tartine is a tart, and while many are made on a pastry crust, others, like this one, are on crusty slices of toast and will remind you of an open-faced sandwich. Be sure to serve it on a plate, with a fork, so you can easily enjoy each bite, and accompany it with a glass of wine.

1. Preheat the toaster oven to 375°F.

2. Place the red pepper and red onion in a medium bowl. Drizzle with 1 tablespoon of the olive oil and season with salt and pepper; toss to coat well. Arrange the red pepper and onion slices in an ungreased 12 x 12-inch baking pan. Bake, uncovered, for 10 minutes.

3. Place the mushrooms and asparagus pieces in that same bowl. Drizzle with the remaining tablespoon of olive oil and season with salt and pepper. Stir the roasted pepper and onion and add the asparagus and mushrooms to the pan. Bake for 7 to 9 minutes or until the vegetables are tender. Remove the baking pan from the toaster oven and set aside.

4. Meanwhile, stir the butter, garlic, and rosemary in a small bowl. Season with salt and pepper and set aside.

5. Toast the bread in the toaster oven. Spread one side of each slice of toast with the butter mixture. Place the toast, buttered side up, on a baking pan. Arrange the vegetables equally on the toast, then top with the cheese.

6. Preheat the toaster oven on Broil. Broil the tartines for 1 to 2 minutes, or just until the cheese melts. Garnish with parsley. Serve warm.

Hot Italian-Style Sub

3 Italian-style hoagie rolls

3 tablespoons unsalted butter, softened

1 teaspoon Italian seasoning

½ teaspoon garlic powder

9 slices salami

12 slices pepperoni

3 thin slices ham

3 tablespoons giardiniera mix, chopped

6 tablespoons shredded mozzarella cheese

CONVECTION OVEN VARIATION: Prepare the recipe as directed, assembling the sandwich. Bake the sandwich on the Convection Oven setting at 350°F for 8 to 10 minutes or until hot throughout and the cheese is melted.

We like to keep hoagie buns in the freezer for go-to sandwich meals in a snap. This sandwich is a meal on its own, or slice each baked sandwich in half and serve with a chopped Italian salad.

1. Preheat the toaster oven to 350°F. Split the rolls lengthwise, cutting almost but not quite though the roll. Place the sandwiches in a 12 x 12-inch baking pan, side by side with the open side face up.

2. Combine the butter, Italian seasoning, and garlic powder in a small bowl. Spread evenly on the inside of the hoagie rolls.

3. Layer a third of the salami, pepperoni, and ham on each sandwich. Sprinkle with the giardiniera mix and mozzarella cheese.

4. Bake for 10 to 15 minutes or until heated through and the cheese is melted.

TIP: Any combination of deli meats can be substituted to make a hot sub sandwich in minutes using your toaster oven.

Toasted Cheese Sandwich

SERVES 1

No need to dirty a skillet when you can easily pop this sandwich into the toaster oven and have golden perfection in a matter of minutes. Refer to the tip to move this up a notch to an adult version.

1. Place a baking pan into the toaster oven and preheat with the baking pan in the oven to 450°F (not the Toast setting).

2. Spread one side of each slice of bread with the butter. Place one piece of bread, buttered side down, on a plate and top with the cheese slices. (Do not allow any cheese to hang over the edge of the bread.) Top with the second slice bread, buttered side up.

3. Carefully remove the hot baking pan from the toaster oven and place the sandwich in the middle of the pan. Bake for 4 minutes. Carefully remove the pan and flip the sandwich, using a spatula. Bake for an additional 3 to 4 minutes, or until the sandwich is golden brown and the cheese is melted.

4. Cool slightly and cut in half for serving.

TIP: Adult versions of this sandwich can easily be created by adding arugula, red onion, or prosciutto. Use goat cheese, Muenster, or a combination of cheeses to up the flavor.

2 slices bread, country, sourdough, white, or your choice

2 teaspoons salted butter, softened

2 to 3 slices cheese such as Colby Jack or cheddar

CONVECTION OVEN VARIATION: Prepare the recipe as directed, assembling the sandwich. Bake the sandwich on the Convection Oven setting at 450°F for 3 minutes. Flip and bake for an additional 2 to 4 minutes, or until the sandwich is golden brown and the cheese is melted.

Bacon Chicken Ranch Sandwiches

SERVES 2

Sandwiches are toasted in a matter of minutes and there is no more need to worry about burning in a hot skillet. Imagine the sandwich possibilities. Feel free to be creative and create your own signature version of a ranch sandwich, too.

1. Preheat the toaster oven to 375°F. Spray a small baking sheet with nonstick cooking spray.

2. Place the chicken tenders on the prepared baking sheet. Bake, uncovered, for 12 to 15 minutes or until the chicken is done and a meat thermometer registers 165°F. Carefully remove from the oven and allow the chicken tenders to cool slightly.

3. Increase the toaster oven temperature to 450°F. Place a 12 x 12-inch baking pan in the toaster oven while it is preheating.

4. Spread one side of each slice of bread with butter. Place two pieces of bread, buttered side down, on a sheet of parchment or wax paper. Spread each slice with 1 tablespoon ranch dressing. Divide the chicken tenders among the two slices. Cut the cheese to fit on the chicken tenders and within the bread perimeter. Fold the slices of bacon to fit within the bread perimeter. Top with the second slice of bread, butter side up.

5. Carefully remove the hot baking pan from the toaster oven and place the sandwiches on the baking sheet. Place the baking sheet in the toaster oven and bake for 4 minutes. Carefully remove the pan and flip the sandwich, using a spatula. Bake for an additional 3 to 4 minutes, or until the sandwich is golden brown and the cheese is melted.

6. Cool slightly and cut in half for serving.

Nonstick cooking spray

½ pound chicken tenders (about 4)

4 slices country or sourdough bread

2 tablespoons unsalted or salted butter, softened

2 tablespoons ranch dressing

2 slices sliced Colby Jack or cheddar cheese

6 slices bacon, cooked until crisp

CONVECTION OVEN VARIATION: Prepare the recipe as directed. Bake the chicken tenders on the Convection Oven setting at 375°F for 10 to 12 minutes, or until the chicken is done and a meat thermometer registers 165°F. Assemble the sandwich as directed. Bake the sandwich on the Convection Oven setting at 450°F for 3 minutes, flip the sandwich, and bake for an additional 2 to 3 minutes, or until the sandwich is golden brown and the cheese is melted.

5

APPETIZERS
+
SNACKS

Firecracker Bites

1 sleeve saltine crackers
(about 43)

¼ cup canola or vegetable oil

1 tablespoon dried parsley
flakes

1 teaspoon dried dill

1 teaspoon garlic powder or
granulated garlic

1 teaspoon onion powder

½ teaspoon freshly ground
black pepper

½ teaspoon seasoned salt

2 teaspoons red pepper flakes

**CONVECTION OVEN
VARIATION:** Prepare the
recipe as directed. Bake the
crackers on the Convection
Oven setting at 250°F for
12 to 14 minutes. Cool and
store as directed.

These work well with most any type of cracker, but be aware
that you can't eat just one! Serve these delicious crackers as
a snack or with any of your favorite dips, including the three
hot dips at the end of this chapter.

1. Place the crackers in a zip-top bag.

2. Combine the canola oil, parsley, dill, garlic powder, onion
powder, pepper, salt, and red pepper flakes in a small bowl.
Pour the oil-seasoning mixture over the crackers and turn the
bag over to allow the mixture to permeate all the crackers.
Turn the bag frequently for about 15 minutes.

3. Preheat the toaster oven to 250°F.

4. Place the crackers evenly in a 12 x 12-inch baking pan. Bake
for 15 minutes. Let the crackers cool completely. These will keep
for several weeks in a sealed container.

Bacon Bites

MAKES 6

These are a fun way to jazz up brunch or cocktail hour. The sweet and salty flavors combine to make these appetizers irresistible.

1. Preheat the toaster oven to 350°F. Line a 12 x 12-inch baking pan with aluminum foil.

2. Spread the brown sugar on a large plate. Wrap a bacon slice around each breadstick. Roll the bacon-wrapped breadstick in the brown sugar and press to adhere to the bacon. Place on the prepared pan.

3. Bake for 18 to 20 minutes, or until the bacon is cooked through. Immediately remove and place the warm sticks on wax paper (to prevent sticking). Let cool to room temperature before serving.

½ cup packed dark brown sugar

6 slices bacon

6 very thin breadsticks from a 3-ounce package

CONVECTION OVEN VARIATION: Prepare the recipe as directed. Bake the bacon bites on the Convection Oven setting at 350°F for 14 to 16 minutes, or until the bacon is cooked through. Cool as directed.

Sausage Cheese Pinwheels

MAKES 16

Your guests will think you spent so much time on such a tasty, elegant nosh to go with cocktails when in fact it took you minutes. I keep these in the freezer for impromptu gatherings so they are a great make-ahead recipe, as well.

1. Preheat the toaster oven to 400°F. Grease a 12 x 12-inch baking pan.

2. Unfold the puff pastry on a lightly floured surface and roll into a 10 x 12-inch rectangle. Carefully spread the sausage over the surface of the rectangle to within ½ inch of all four edges. Sprinkle the cheese evenly over the sausage. Starting with the long side, roll up tightly and press the edges to seal.

3. Using a serrated knife, slice the roll into ½-inch-thick pieces. You will get about 16 slices. Place the slices, cut side up, in the prepared baking pan. Bake for 18 to 22 minutes or until golden and the sausage is cooked through.

4. Serve warm or at room temperature.

TIPS: Let the sausage set out of the refrigerator for about an hour before preparing this recipe. This will make it much easier to spread over the pastry sheet.

Assemble these a day ahead, wrap tightly in plastic wrap, and refrigerate. The slicing will be much easier. You can also slice and freeze (cooked or uncooked) for up to 2 months.

VARIATION: Sprinkle the sausage with about 2 tablespoons finely chopped black olives, then top with the shredded cheese.

1 sheet frozen puff pastry, about 9 inches square, thawed (½ of a 17.3-ounce package)

½ pound bulk sausage

¾ cup shredded cheddar cheese

CONVECTION OVEN VARIATION: Prepare the recipe as directed. Bake the sausage cheese rolls on the Convection Oven setting at 400°F for 15 to 18 minutes, or until golden and the sausage is cooked through.

Spicy Pigs in a Blanket

MAKES 32

6 tablespoons unsalted butter, melted

1 teaspoon poppy seeds

1 teaspoon dry minced onion

½ teaspoon granulated garlic

½ teaspoon dry mustard

¼ teaspoon red pepper flakes

1 (8-ounce) tube refrigerated crescent dough sheets

1 (12-ounce) package cocktail smoked sausages

CONVECTION OVEN VARIATION: Prepare the recipe as directed. Bake the pigs in a blanket on the Convection Oven setting at 375°F for 12 to 14 minutes, or until golden brown.

This is a throwback to an ever-popular appetizer. The seasonings bring the flavor up a notch and guarantees that this will be a hit at any party or gathering.

1. Combine the butter, poppy seeds, onion, garlic, dry mustard, and red pepper flakes in a small bowl.

2. Lightly flour a clean surface and unroll the crescent roll sheet. Cut the sheet in half down the center, then cut those pieces in half the other way. Continue to make vertical and horizontal cuts until you have 32 strips of dough.

3. Preheat the toaster oven to 375°F.

4. Drain and pat dry the cocktail sausages using paper towels. Wrap each sausage in a strip of dough. Place about half on a 12 x 12-inch baking pan, seam side down.

5. Stir the butter mixture again to distribute all the spices and brush generously over the pastry-wrapped sausages. Bake for 14 to 15 minutes, or until they are golden brown. Repeat with the remaining half of the ingredients. Allow to cool slightly before serving.

TIPS: These are packed with flavor on their own, but you may want to serve with a spicy mustard on the side.

If desired, substitute a tube of crescent rolls for the crescent roll sheets. Unroll the dough and pinch the perforations together to seal, making sheets. Proceed as the recipe directs.

Sweet Chili–Glazed Wings

SERVES 4

These wings are just sweet and spicy enough to become a crowd favorite. They would be great for any gathering, but we think every time friends crowd around your television to cheer on your favorite team, you need to make a batch of these. Go Kansas City Chiefs!

1. Place the chicken drumettes in a deep bowl. Stir the soy sauce, honey, rice vinegar, sesame oil, chili garlic paste, and pepper in a small bowl. Pour the soy sauce mixture over the chicken. Cover the bowl and refrigerate for several hours or overnight.

2. Preheat the toaster oven to 375°F. Line a 12 x 12-inch baking pan with aluminum foil.

3. Drain and discard the marinade. Pat the chicken dry and arrange in a single layer in the prepared pan. Bake, uncovered, for 18 to 20 minutes or until lightly browned and almost done.

4. Brush the chicken with the sweet chili sauce, turning to coat evenly. Bake for 6 to 7 minutes or until the chicken is done, a meat thermometer registers 165°F, and the edges are beginning to crisp.

TIPS: The drumettes are everyone's favorite, but if desired, use a combination of drumettes and wingettes. If you purchase chicken wings, cut the wings at the joints and discard the tips.

What is sweet chili sauce? There is a wide array of chili sauce on the market, and sometimes it might be a little confusing. For this recipe, the sweet chili sauce, also called Thai or Asian sweet chili sauce, is typically shelved with the Asian ingredients in larger grocery stores. It is commonly made with rice wine and red chili peppers, and is not the tomato-based sauce we of the Midwest grew up with.

1 pound chicken wing drumettes

½ cup reduced-sodium soy sauce

3 tablespoons honey

3 tablespoons unseasoned rice vinegar

1 tablespoon sesame oil

1½ teaspoons chili garlic paste

¼ teaspoon freshly ground black pepper

¼ cup jarred Asian sweet chili sauce (see tips)

CONVECTION OVEN VARIATION: Prepare the recipe as directed. Bake the wings on the Convection Oven setting at 375°F for 15 minutes. Brush the chicken with the sauce and bake for 5 minutes or until the chicken is done, a meat thermometer registers 165°F, and the edges are beginning to crisp.

Hot Bacon-Cheese Dip

MAKES ABOUT 3 CUPS

Nonstick cooking spray

1 (8-ounce) package cream cheese, cut into cubes and softened

1 cup sour cream

2 tablespoons whole milk

1 tablespoon Worcestershire sauce

¼ teaspoon Sriracha or hot sauce

10 strips bacon, cooked until crisp and crumbled

8 ounces shredded sharp cheddar cheese

1 green onion, white and green portions, thinly sliced

Tortilla chips, crackers, broccoli or cauliflower florets, or other favorites, for dipping

This may become your favorite go-to hot dip. It's ideal to serve while watching the game or anytime friends gather for a casual evening. Serve this delicious dip with your favorite chips, crackers, or vegetables, and enjoy.

1. Preheat the toaster oven to 350°F. Spray a 1-quart casserole dish with nonstick cooking spray.

2. Stir the cream cheese, sour cream, milk, Worcestershire sauce, and Sriracha in a medium bowl. Blend well.

3. Reserve 2 tablespoon crumbled bacon for the garnish. Stir the remaining bacon and the cheddar cheese into the cream cheese mixture. Spoon into the prepared dish and cover.

4. Bake for 20 minutes. Stir the dip, cover, and bake for an additional 10 minutes or until hot and melted. Garnish with the reserved bacon and green onion.

5. Serve warm with any of your favorites for dipping.

Baked Spinach + Artichoke Dip

MAKES ABOUT 5 CUPS

Nonstick cooking spray

2 tablespoons unsalted butter

½ medium onion, chopped

2 cloves garlic, minced

5 ounces frozen, chopped loose-pack spinach (about 1¾ cups), thawed and squeezed dry

1 (13.75-ounce) can quartered artichoke hearts, drained and chopped

1 (8-ounce) package cream cheese, cut into cubes and softened

½ cup mayonnaise

Kosher salt and freshly ground black pepper

2 cups shredded Colby Jack or Mexican blend cheese

¾ cup shredded Parmesan cheese

Tortilla chips, pita bread triangles, carrot or celery sticks, broccoli or cauliflower florets, for dipping

Is this your favorite restaurant-style appetizer? It sure is a popular one. This recipe lets you vary the amount of spinach so your dip is perfect for your tastes. Serve it with your favorite dippers—are they tortilla chips, pita bread triangles, or vegetables? The choice is yours.

1. Preheat the toaster oven to 350°F. Spray a 2-quart casserole dish with nonstick cooking spray.

2. Melt the butter in a large skillet over medium-high heat. Add the onion and cook, stirring frequently, until tender, 3 to 5 minutes. Add the garlic and cook, stirring frequently, for 30 seconds. Remove from the heat.

3. Stir in the spinach, artichokes, cream cheese, and mayonnaise. Season with salt and pepper. Blend in the Colby Jack and Parmesan cheeses. Spoon the mixture into the prepared casserole dish. Cover and bake for 20 minutes. Stir the dip and bake, covered, for an additional 10 to 15 minutes, or until hot and melted. Serve with any of the dipping choices.

TIP: Frozen spinach is now readily available as bags of chopped spinach or the classic (10-ounce) box of chopped spinach. For ease, the recipe lists the loose-pack frozen chopped spinach. If you like spinach, feel free to increase the amount to 8 to 10 ounces of chopped spinach or substitute one (10-ounce) package frozen chopped spinach.

Caramelized Onion Dip

MAKES ABOUT 2½ CUPS

This is the dip to serve on a winter's eve with a glass of wine. It is so good it just might replace dinner.

1. Melt the butter and olive oil in a large skillet over medium heat. Add the onion and season with salt. Cook, stirring frequently, for 3 minutes. Reduce the heat to low and cook, stirring occasionally, for 20 to 25 minutes, or until the onions are a deep golden brown color.

2. Increase the heat to medium. Stir in the garlic, wine, thyme, and pepper. Cook, stirring frequently, for 3 minutes or until the wine has mostly evaporated. Remove from the heat.

3. Meanwhile, toast the baguette slices in the toaster oven until golden brown and crisp; set aside.

4. Preheat the toaster oven to 350°F. Spray a 1-quart casserole with nonstick cooking spray.

5. Stir the Gruyère, sour cream, mayonnaise, Parmesan, and bacon into the onions. Spoon the mixture into the prepared casserole dish. Cover and bake for 20 minutes or until hot and the cheese is melted. Allow to stand for 5 to 10 minutes before serving. To serve, spoon the warm onion-cheese mixture onto the toast.

TIP: If you prefer, substitute chicken or vegetable broth for the white wine.

1 tablespoon unsalted butter

1 tablespoon olive oil

1 large sweet onion, quartered and very thinly sliced crosswise

Kosher salt

1 clove garlic, minced

3 tablespoons dry white wine

½ teaspoon dried thyme leaves

½ teaspoon freshly ground black pepper

1 baguette, thinly sliced

Nonstick cooking spray

1 cup shredded Gruyère or Swiss cheese

½ cup sour cream

½ cup mayonnaise

¼ cup shredded Parmesan cheese

3 strips bacon, cooked until crisp and crumbled

6

SIDE DISHES

Rosemary Roasted Vegetables

3 tablespoons olive oil

Grated zest and juice of
1 lemon

2 tablespoons chopped fresh
rosemary leaves

4 cloves garlic, minced

Kosher salt and freshly
ground black pepper

6 cups vegetables, diced,
such as bell peppers,
onions, zucchini,
mushrooms, cherry
tomatoes, potatoes,
and eggplant

**CONVECTION OVEN
VARIATION:** Prepare the
recipe as directed. Roast on
the Convection Oven setting
at 425°F for 10 minutes. Stir
and roast for an additional
8 to 13 minutes, or until the
vegetables are tender.

This recipe will please even the finickiest vegetable eater.
This is a perfect way to use whatever fresh vegetables
are hiding in the refrigerator. Create a great side dish to
complement grilled meat, or simply toss with pasta for
a vegetarian meal in minutes. (See photo on page 107.)

1. Preheat the toaster oven to 425°F.

2. Stir the olive oil, lemon zest, lemon juice, rosemary, and
garlic in a small bowl. Season with salt and pepper. Place the
vegetables into a large bowl and drizzle the olive oil mixture
over all. Stir gently to coat.

3. Arrange the vegetables in a single layer in a 12 x 12-inch baking
pan. Roast for 10 minutes. Stir and roast for an additional 10 to
15 minutes, or until the vegetables are tender.

Mustard Green Beans with Walnuts

SERVES 4

These rich and tangy green beans are delicious, and they're good for you, too. Make them when you want a change from your old-fashioned green bean recipe. These are best served at room temperature, but are tasty enough to enjoy straight from the refrigerator. (See photo on page 86.)

1. Preheat the toaster oven to 425°F. Place the green beans in a large bowl and spray with nonstick cooking spray. Season with salt and pepper. Place the green beans in a 12 x 12-inch baking pan.

2. Roast for 10 minutes. Stir and roast for an additional 10 minutes, or until the green beans are the desired tenderness.

3. Meanwhile, whisk the vinegar and shallots in a large bowl. Let stand while the green beans are roasting. Whisk the mustard into the vinegar mixture. Stir in the honey. Gradually add the olive oil, whisking until the mixture is thick. Add the green beans; toss gently to coat. Season to taste with additional salt and pepper, if needed. Sprinkle with the walnuts. Serve at room temperature

TIPS: If you prefer, omit the nonstick cooking spray and toss the green beans with 1 tablespoon olive oil. Season with salt and pepper and proceed as the recipe directs.

Toasting nuts intensifies their flavor and is easy to do in your toaster oven. See page 13.

1½ pounds fresh green beans, trimmed

Nonstick cooking spray

Kosher salt and freshly ground black pepper

1½ tablespoons white wine vinegar

2 tablespoons finely chopped shallots

1½ tablespoons Dijon mustard

1 teaspoon honey

2 tablespoons extra-virgin olive oil

⅓ cup coarsely chopped walnuts, toasted

CONVECTION OVEN VARIATION: Prepare the recipe as directed. Roast on the Convection Oven setting at 425°F for 8 minutes. Stir and roast for an additional 8 to 11 minutes, or until the beans are the desired tenderness. Proceed as the recipe directs.

Loaded Cauliflower Casserole

SERVES 6 TO 8

Nonstick cooking spray

1 cup heavy cream

4 tablespoons unsalted butter

3 cloves garlic, minced

1 teaspoon fresh thyme leaves

¾ teaspoon kosher salt

¼ teaspoon freshly ground black pepper

6 cups cauliflower florets (a medium head)

½ cup finely chopped sweet or yellow onion

2 cups shredded white cheddar cheese

1½ cups fresh coarse bread crumbs

2 tablespoons sesame seeds

3 tablespoons unsalted butter, melted

CONVECTION OVEN VARIATION: Prepare the recipe as directed. Bake on the Convection Oven setting at 425°F for 18 to 20 minutes, or until the cauliflower is tender. Uncover and bake for an additional 13 to 14 minutes, or until the top is bubbly and beginning to turn golden. Prepare the bread crumbs as directed and sprinkle over the top. Bake for an additional 10 to 12 minutes or until golden.

Step aside, scalloped potatoes, this cauliflower concoction will be the new star of the side dish show. It is perfect to serve with grilled steaks and a salad. A great recipe to have in your collection for entertaining friends and family.

1. Preheat the toaster oven to 425°F. Spray a 9-inch deep-dish pie plate or 9-inch cake pan with nonstick cooking spray.

2. Bring the cream, butter, garlic, thyme, salt, and pepper to a simmer in a small saucepan over medium heat. Remove from the heat.

3. Place half of the cauliflower into the prepared pan. Sprinkle with half of the onion and half of the cheese. Repeat with the remaining cauliflower, onion, and cheese. Pour the cream mixture over all. Cover and bake until the cauliflower is tender and cooked through, about 20 minutes.

4. Remove the foil and bake for an additional 15 minutes, or until the top is bubbly and beginning to turn golden.

5. Combine the bread crumbs, sesame seeds, and melted butter in a small bowl. Sprinkle over the top and bake for an additional 15 minutes or until golden.

TIPS: You can bake this ahead; cover and refrigerate. Place in the toaster oven at 400°F to reheat until bubbling.

Of course, you can substitute shredded sharp cheddar cheese, in the familiar yellow color, for the white cheddar listed in this recipe.

VARIATION: This side dish is equally delicious if prepared with half cauliflower and half broccoli. Proceed as the recipe directs.

Roasted Brussels Sprouts Au Gratin

SERVES 6

Au gratin means topped with cheese, and for most of us, that simply means it is a delicious, cheesy recipe. Add crisp bacon, and those Brussels sprouts become an unbeatable side dish.

1. Preheat the toaster oven to 450°F.

2. Toss the Brussels sprouts with the olive oil in a large bowl. Season with salt and pepper. Arrange the Brussels sprouts in a single layer in a 12 x 12-inch baking pan. Bake uncovered for 10 minutes. Stir and bake for an additional 8 to 10 minutes, or until the edges are beginning to char and the Brussels sprouts are just tender. Remove from the oven.

3. Reduce the toaster oven to 375°F. Spray a 1½-quart casserole dish or an 8 x 8-inch square baking pan with nonstick cooking spray. Place the Brussels sprouts in the casserole dish. Sprinkle with the crisp bacon.

4. Melt 2 tablespoons of the butter in a small saucepan over medium heat. Stir in the flour, blending until smooth and cook, stirring constantly, for 1 minute. Gradually add the milk and cook, stirring constantly, until the mixture is bubbly and thickened. Season with salt and pepper. Stir in the cheese and thyme and cook, stirring until melted. Pour the sauce over the Brussels sprouts.

5. Melt the remaining tablespoon of butter. Stir in the panko bread crumbs and Parmesan cheese. Sprinkle the bread crumb mixture over the casserole. Bake, uncovered, for 15 minutes or until golden brown and the edges are bubbling.

1 pound fresh Brussels sprouts, trimmed and halved

2 tablespoons olive oil

Kosher salt and freshly ground black pepper

Nonstick cooking spray

2 slices bacon, cooked until crisp and crumbled

3 tablespoons unsalted butter

2 tablespoons all-purpose flour

1 cup whole milk

1 cup shredded Gruyère or Swiss cheese

½ teaspoon dried thyme leaves

¼ cup panko bread crumbs

¼ cup shredded Parmesan cheese

CONVECTION OVEN VARIATION: Prepare the recipe as directed. Bake on the Convection Oven setting at 450°F for 8 minutes. Stir and bake for an additional 7 to 9 minutes, or until the edges are beginning to char and the Brussels sprouts are just tender. Proceed and prepare the casserole as directed. Bake for 12 to 14 minutes or until golden brown and the edges are bubbling.

Roasted Fennel with Wine + Parmesan

SERVES 3

3 medium fennel bulbs, trimmed, cored, and cut horizontally into ⅓-inch-thick slices, reserving 2 teaspoons fronds (leaves)

2½ tablespoons olive oil, plus more for greasing

Kosher salt and freshly ground black pepper

2 tablespoons dry white wine

3 tablespoons shredded Parmesan cheese

CONVECTION OVEN VARIATION: Prepare the recipe as directed. Roast on the Convection Oven setting at 425°F for 10 minutes. Stir and continue to roast for 8 to 10 minutes, or until the fennel is brown and crisp around the edges and the largest piece is tender when pierced with the tip of a knife. Drizzle with the wine and sprinkle with the Parmesan cheese as directed. Bake for an additional 1 to 2 minutes or until the cheese is melted. Proceed as the recipe directs.

Are you a fan of fennel? We are, and we think it is so good it should become a vegetable rock star, much like kale recently has become. Fennel tastes fresh and has an aromatic anise flavor. We enjoy it raw, sautéed, roasted, and added to soups and sauces. Fennel, a member of the carrot family, is low in calories and high in nutrients, and once you taste this delicious recipe, you will want to serve it often. (See photo on page 120.)

1. Preheat the toaster oven to 425°F. Lightly oil a 12 x 12-inch baking pan.

2. Arrange the fennel in a single layer on the prepared pan. Drizzle the olive oil evenly over and season with salt and pepper. Stir to blend well and arrange in a single layer. Roast for 12 minutes. Stir and roast for an additional 10 to 12 minutes, or until the fennel is brown and crisp around the edges and the largest piece is tender when pierced with the tip of a knife.

3. Carefully remove the pan from the oven. Drizzle the wine over the cooked fennel and sprinkle with the Parmesan cheese. Return to the oven and bake for an additional 2 minutes or until the cheese is melted. Sprinkle with the reserved fronds before serving warm.

TIP: We always have extra white wine in the refrigerator, and this is an excellent use for adding flavor to many dishes. If you do not have wine on hand or prefer not to use it, just omit this step.

The bright green feathery fennel leaves are known as fronds and add a bright flavor. Snip or cut the fronds from the celery-like stalk to use in this recipe.

Sage Butter Roasted Butternut Squash with Pepitas

SERVES 4

Butternut squash slices make this dish look distinctive. When purchasing the squash, look for one that has an elongated neck so you can cut several whole slices from the squash.

1. Preheat the toaster oven to 375°F. Spray a 12 x 12-inch baking pan with nonstick cooking spray.

2. Cut the squash crosswise into ¾-inch slices. Use a teaspoon to remove the seeds, as needed, from the center of the slices. Arrange the slices in a single layer on the baking sheet.

3. Stir the butter, sage, honey, and pumpkin seeds in a small bowl. Season with salt and pepper. Spoon the butter mixture over the squash slices, then brush to coat each slice of squash evenly.

4. Roast for 20 minutes or until the squash is tender. Transfer to a serving platter and spoon the seeds and any drippings over the squash. Garnish with extra sage leaves, if desired.

TIP: To make the squash easier to slice, prick the squash in several spots with the tip of a sharp knife. Microwave the whole squash on High (100 percent) power for 1 to 2 minutes, then let stand for 3 minutes. Choose a sharp, heavy knife to cut off the stems. Peel, then slice the squash.

Nonstick cooking spray

1 medium butternut squash, peeled

2 tablespoons unsalted butter, melted

2 tablespoons minced fresh sage, plus more leaves for garnish (optional)

1 teaspoon honey

¼ cup shelled pumpkin seeds, or pepitas

Kosher salt and freshly ground black pepper

CONVECTION OVEN VARIATION: Prepare the recipe as directed. Roast the squash on the Convection Oven setting at 375°F for 16 to 18 minutes or until the squash is tender. Proceed as the recipe directs.

Oven-Baked Farro with Vegetables

SERVES 6

Nonstick cooking spray

2 tablespoons olive oil

½ medium red onion, chopped

½ medium red bell pepper, chopped

1 carrot, chopped

2 cloves garlic, minced

Kosher salt and freshly ground black pepper

½ cup pearled farro, rinsed and drained

1 (14.5-ounce) can diced tomatoes, with liquid

2 teaspoons white wine vinegar

2 tablespoons minced fresh basil or flat-leaf (Italian) parsley

Farro is increasing in popularity, and it's no wonder. A form of wheat, farro's chewy, nutty flavor is captivating. This side dish combines the farro with sautéed vegetables so it becomes a tasty side dish for any grilled or roasted meat. The farro in this recipe is pearled, which means that the outer bran has been removed so it cooks more quickly than whole farro.

1. Preheat the toaster oven to 375°F. Spray a 2-quart casserole with nonstick cooking spray.

2. Heat the olive oil in a large skillet over medium-high heat. Add the onion, bell pepper, and carrot and cook, stirring frequently, for 3 to 5 minutes, or until the vegetables are tender. Stir in the garlic and cook for 30 seconds. Season with salt and pepper.

3. Stir in the farro and cook, stirring frequently, until the farro is toasted and golden brown. Stir in the tomatoes, vinegar, and 2 tablespoons water. Spoon into the prepared casserole dish. Cover and bake for 45 to 55 minutes or until the farro is tender.

4. Sprinkle with the basil just before serving.

TIP: If you desire, substitute a 9 x 5-inch loaf pan for the 2-quart baking pan listed in this recipe.

Parmesan Garlic French Fries

SERVES 4

- 16 ounces frozen regular-cut french fries
- 2 tablespoons olive oil
- 1 teaspoon Italian seasoning
- ½ teaspoon garlic powder
- ½ teaspoon kosher salt
- ¼ teaspoon freshly ground black pepper
- ¼ cup grated Parmesan cheese
- 2 tablespoons minced fresh flat-leaf (Italian) parsley

CONVECTION OVEN SETTING: Prepare the recipe as directed. Bake the fries on the Convection Oven setting at 425°F for 9 minutes. Stir and bake for an additional 8 to 13 minutes, or until the fries are golden brown and crisp. Proceed as the recipe directs.

Now your family can enjoy a delicious batch of french fries with the perfect blend of garlic and Parmesan cheese. The best news is that this recipe begins with frozen french fries, which is ideal, since they taste so good. They will quickly become a family favorite. (See photo on page 114.)

1. Preheat the toaster oven to 425°F. Line a 12 x 12-inch baking pan with nonstick aluminum foil (or if lining the pan with regular foil, spray it with nonstick cooking spray).

2. Place the french fries in a large bowl. Drizzle with the olive oil and toss to coat the fries evenly.

3. Blend the Italian seasoning, garlic powder, salt, and pepper in a small bowl. Sprinkle the seasonings over the fries and toss to coat evenly. Spread the fries in a single layer in the prepared pan.

4. Bake, uncovered, for 10 minutes. Stir and bake for an additional 10 to 15 minutes, or until the fries are golden brown and crisp.

5. Remove the fries from the oven and immediately sprinkle with the Parmesan cheese and parsley. Toss gently to coat them evenly.

TIP: Parmesan cheese is readily available in many forms, including a wedge or block, shredded, and grated. The best flavor will come if you freshly grate the cheese, and for this recipe, grate it finely so it will melt quickly when you sprinkle it over the hot fries. If you would rather not grate the cheese for the fries, select grated Parmesan cheese that is sold in the refrigerator or deli case of the grocery store. The flavor of the refrigerated variety will far exceed the canned variety you once might have been tempted to buy.

Cranberry Pecan Rice Pilaf

SERVES 8

Fall breezes outside mean it is the perfect time to serve this rice pilaf. Are you hosting the family holiday feast? That probably means the big oven will be filled with the turkey, ham, or roast, so this side dish is ideal for the toaster oven.

1. Preheat the toaster oven to 375°F. Spray a 2-quart casserole with nonstick cooking spray.

2. Melt the butter in a large skillet over medium-high heat. Add the shallot and cook, stirring frequently, for 3 minutes. Stir in the rice and cook, stirring frequently, until the rice is beginning to toast. Stir in the pecans and cook until the rice is golden brown and the pecans are toasted. Stir in the broth and 1/3 cup water. Heat until it just begins to boil. Remove from the heat and stir in the cranberries, parsley, and rosemary. Season with salt and pepper. Spoon the rice mixture into the prepared casserole dish.

3. Cover and bake for 70 to 75 minutes or until the rice is tender.

TIP: If you desire, substitute a 9 x 5-inch loaf pan for the 2-quart baking pan listed in this recipe.

Nonstick cooking spray

2 tablespoons unsalted butter

1 shallot, chopped

2/3 cup long-grain brown rice, rinsed and drained

1/4 cup chopped pecans

1 (14.5-ounce) can reduced-sodium chicken broth

1/2 cup dried sweetened cranberries

2 tablespoons minced fresh flat-leaf (Italian) parsley

1 tablespoon minced fresh rosemary leaves or 1 teaspoon dried rosemary leaves, crumbled

Kosher salt and freshly ground black pepper

7

SHEET PAN DINNERS

Honey-Glazed Ginger Pork Meatballs

Once you taste the sauce that envelops these meatballs, you will be making a long list of other ways to serve it. The sauce alone delivers just the right sweet-sour flavor that we all crave.

1. Preheat the toaster oven to 375°F. Line a 12 x 12-inch baking pan with nonstick aluminum foil (or if lining the pan with regular foil, spray it with nonstick cooking spray).

2. Combine the pork, onion, garlic, ginger, sesame oil, egg, and panko bread crumbs in a large bowl. Season with salt and pepper. Form into meatballs about 1½ inches in diameter. Place the meatballs in the prepared baking pan. Bake for 18 to 20 minutes or until done and a meat thermometer registers 160°F.

3. Make the Honey Ginger Sauce: Combine the sesame oil, canola oil, garlic, and ginger in a medium skillet over medium-high heat. Cook, stirring frequently, for 1 minute. Add the vinegar, soy sauce, honey, and chili sauce and bring to a boil. Whisk the cornstarch with the water in a small bowl. Stir the cornstarch mixture into the sauce and cook, stirring constantly, until thickened. Add the meatballs to the skillet and coat with the sauce. Sprinkle with the cilantro for serving.

TIP: Fresh ginger adds a bright flavor to so many recipes. Purchase a large piece of ginger and peel the entire piece. Grate what you need for this recipe, then place the leftover knob of ginger in a freezer bag and freeze for future use. You can even grate the frozen ginger; no need to thaw it first.

1½ pounds ground pork

2 tablespoons finely chopped onion

3 cloves garlic, minced

1 teaspoon minced fresh ginger

1 teaspoon sesame oil

1 large egg

3 tablespoons panko bread crumbs

Kosher salt and freshly ground black pepper

HONEY GINGER SAUCE

2 tablespoons sesame oil

1 tablespoon canola or vegetable oil

3 cloves garlic, minced

1½ tablespoons minced fresh ginger

3 tablespoons unseasoned rice wine vinegar

1 tablespoon reduced-sodium soy sauce

3 tablespoons honey

2 to 3 teaspoons garlic chili sauce

1 teaspoon cornstarch

1 tablespoon cold water

2 tablespoons minced fresh cilantro

Middle Eastern Roasted Chicken

SERVES 4

3 tablespoons fresh lemon juice

¼ cup plus 1 tablespoon olive oil

4 cloves garlic, minced

½ teaspoon kosher salt

1 teaspoon freshly ground black pepper

1 teaspoon ground cumin

1 teaspoon paprika

½ teaspoon turmeric

⅛ teaspoon red pepper flakes

1 pound boneless, skinless chicken breasts

1 large onion, cut into thin wedges

CONVECTION OVEN VARIATION: Prepare the recipe as directed. Roast the chicken and onions on the Convection Oven setting at 425°F for 18 to 20 minutes, or until the chicken is done and a meat thermometer registers 165°F. Proceed as the recipe directs.

This is perfect to serve with pita bread, diced cucumbers and tomatoes, feta crumbles, hummus, or rice. You can make this into a pita wrap for patio dining.

1. Whisk the lemon juice, ¼ cup olive oil, garlic, salt, pepper, cumin, paprika, turmeric, and red pepper flakes in a small bowl until blended.

2. Cut the chicken breast lengthwise into thin scaloppine slices. Place the chicken in a nonreactive dish and pour the marinade over the chicken. Turn the chicken to coat thoroughly and evenly. Cover, refrigerate, and marinate for at least 1 hour and up to 10 hours. (The longer the better, as the flavor melds with the chicken.)

3. Remove the chicken from the refrigerator and add the onion to the marinade.

4. Preheat the toaster oven to 425°F. Brush the remaining tablespoon of olive oil over the bottom of a 12 x 12-inch pan. Place the chicken pieces on one side of the baking sheet and the onion wedges on the other side in a single layer. Discard any remaining marinade.

5. Roast for 20 to 25 minutes or until the chicken is browned and a meat thermometer registers 165°F. Remove from the oven and let rest a few minutes, then slice the chicken into thin strips. Toss with the onion and serve.

TIP: If you do not want to purchase all the spices listed, you could purchase a package of chicken shawarma seasoning mix. Look for it at markets that specialize in Middle Eastern foods. Use 1 tablespoon of the mix in this recipe in place of the seasonings listed.

Roasted Harissa Chicken + Vegetables

SERVES 4

Nonstick cooking spray

1 medium zucchini, halved lengthwise and sliced crosswise ½ inch thick

½ large red onion, sliced ¼ inch thick

2 tablespoons olive oil

Kosher salt and freshly ground black pepper

1 pound boneless, skinless chicken breasts, cut into 1-inch cubes

½ teaspoon ground cumin

1 clove garlic, minced

2 tablespoons harissa sauce or paste

1 tablespoon honey

2 tablespoons minced fresh cilantro

2 cups hot cooked rice

Optional toppings: plain Greek yogurt or sour cream, sesame seeds (toasted or chopped), or dry-roasted peanuts

CONVECTION OVEN VARIATION: Prepare the recipe as directed. Roast the vegetables on the Convection Oven setting at 400°F for 8 minutes. Add the chicken and roast for 8 to 9 minutes. Brush with the sauce and roast for an additional 7 to 9 minutes, or until the vegetables are tender and the chicken is done.

Just a touch of heat describes this chicken and vegetable sheet pan dinner. Harissa is a chili pepper paste common in Africa. It is increasingly popular in the United States, and jars of sauce or paste are often sold in larger grocery stores. If you are not familiar with it, try it now. While this dish is not overly spicy, you might try preparing it first with about half the amount of harissa listed in the recipe.

1. Preheat the toaster oven to 400°F. Spray a 12 x 12-inch baking pan with nonstick cooking spray.

2. Place the zucchini and red onion in a medium bowl. Drizzle with 1 tablespoon olive oil and season with salt and pepper. Stir to coat the vegetables evenly. Arrange the vegetables in a single layer in the prepared baking pan. Roast, uncovered, for 10 minutes.

3. Place the chicken cubes in that same bowl. Drizzle with the remaining 1 tablespoon olive oil. Season with the cumin, garlic, salt, and pepper. Stir to coat the chicken evenly.

4. Stir the vegetables and move to one side of the pan. Arrange the chicken in a single layer on the other side of the pan. Roast for 10 minutes.

5. Blend the harissa and honey in a small bowl. Drizzle the sauce over the chicken and vegetables. Using a pastry brush, coat the chicken and vegetables evenly. Roast, uncovered, for an additional 8 to 10 minutes, or until the vegetables are tender and the chicken registers 165°F on a meat thermometer.

6. Spoon the chicken, vegetables, and any collected liquid onto a serving platter. Sprinkle with the cilantro. Serve the chicken and vegetables with the rice and, if desired, a dollop of plain Greek yogurt and a sprinkling of sesame seeds.

Miso-Glazed Salmon with Broccoli

We have developed a real love of miso, and if you haven't tried it, now is the perfect time. The fermented soybean paste adds a depth of delicious flavor to this fish. Combine the salty flavor of miso with the mirin, which is sweet rice wine, and you have the basis for this sweet-salty-spicy glaze. Add the broccoli, and in just minutes a healthy dinner is on the table.

1. Preheat the toaster oven to 425°F. Spray a 12 x 12-inch baking pan with nonstick cooking spray.

2. Stir the miso, mirin, brown sugar, ginger, and sesame oil in a small bowl; set aside.

3. Toss the broccoli spears with the canola oil and season with salt and pepper. Place the broccoli on the pan. Bake, uncovered, for 10 minutes. Stir the broccoli and move to one side of the pan.

4. Place the salmon, skin side down, on the other end of the pan. Brush lightly with olive oil and season with salt and pepper. Bake for 10 minutes.

5. Brush the fish generously with the miso sauce. Bake for an additional 3 to 5 minutes, or until the fish flakes easily with a fork and a meat thermometer registers 145°F.

TIPS: If desired, brush some of the miso mixture over the broccoli when topping the salmon.

Yellow miso, which can actually range in color from yellow to a light brown, is often considered a general-use miso. Red miso has a stronger flavor, while white miso is a little sweet and is perfect in sauces. You will find an array of miso at markets that specialize in Asian foods. Store the miso tightly covered in the refrigerator, and if you remove what you need with a clean spoon, return it to the refrigerator. It will keep for several months.

Don't have miso or mirin? While the flavor won't be quite the same, there are some easy substitutions. For the mirin, dissolve 1½ teaspoons sugar in 2 tablespoons dry sherry, vermouth, or white wine. Instead of the miso, use 1 tablespoon soy sauce.

Nonstick cooking spray

2 tablespoons miso, preferably yellow

2 tablespoons mirin

1 tablespoon packed dark brown sugar

2 teaspoons minced fresh ginger

1½ teaspoons sesame oil

8 ounces fresh broccoli, cut into spears

1 tablespoon canola or vegetable oil

Kosher salt and freshly ground black pepper

2 salmon fillets (5 to 6 ounces each)

CONVECTION OVEN VARIATION: Prepare the recipe as directed. Bake the broccoli on the Convection Oven setting at 425°F for 8 minutes. Add the fish to the pan and bake for 8 minutes. Glaze the fish and bake for an additional 2 to 4 minutes, or until the fish is done and a meat thermometer registers 145°F.

Sheet Pan Beef Fajitas

SERVES 3

The key to this recipe is tossing the cooked beef in the lime juice and garlic just before serving. This flavors the meat and goes nicely with the broiled spiced vegetables. Pass the salsa, guacamole, shredded cheese, and sour cream to complete the meal.

1. Position the rack to broil. Preheat the toaster oven on the Broil setting. Spray a 12 x 12-inch baking pan with nonstick cooking spray.

2. Combine the olive oil, chili powder, cumin, and salt in a small bowl. Add the onion and bell pepper and toss to coat them evenly with the mixture. Use a slotted spoon to remove the vegetables from the seasoned oil mixture. Reserve the seasoned oil mixture. Place the vegetables in a single layer on the prepared pan. Broil for about 5 minutes or until the vegetables are beginning to brown.

3. Meanwhile, toss the steak strips in the reserved seasoned oil mixture. Push the vegetables to one side of the pan and add the steak in a single layer on the other side of the pan. Broil for 5 minutes.

4. When the meat is done, remove the meat from the pan and toss with the lime juice and garlic. Serve the meat and vegetables in warm tortillas.

Nonstick cooking spray

3 tablespoons olive oil

1½ teaspoons chili powder

2 teaspoons ground cumin

1 teaspoon kosher salt

1 onion, halved and sliced into ¼-inch strips

1 large red or green bell pepper, cut into thin strips

¾-pound flank steak, cut across the grain into thin strips

3 tablespoons fresh lime juice

3 cloves garlic, minced

6 flour or corn tortillas, warmed

Sheet Pan Loaded Nachos

SERVES 4

1 tablespoon canola or vegetable oil

½ pound lean ground beef

½ cup chopped onion

2 cloves garlic, minced

1 teaspoon chili powder

½ teaspoon ground cumin

Kosher salt and freshly ground black pepper

6 ounces tortilla chips

½ cup canned black beans, rinsed and drained

1½ cups shredded sharp cheddar cheese or Mexican blend cheese

½ cup salsa

Optional toppings: sliced jalapeño peppers, chopped bell peppers, sliced ripe olives, chopped tomatoes, minced fresh cilantro, sour cream, chopped avocado, guacamole, or chopped onion

Everyone's favorite bar food is as close as your toaster oven. Best of all, you can custom-make the nachos with any of your favorite toppings. Gather your friends and enjoy!

1. Preheat the toaster oven to 400°F. Line a 12 x 12-inch baking pan with nonstick aluminum foil. (Or if lining the pan with regular foil, spray it with nonstick cooking spray.)

2. Heat the oil in a large skillet over medium-high heat. Add the ground beef and onion and cook, stirring frequently, until the beef is almost done. Add the garlic, chili powder, cumin, season with salt and pepper, and cook, stirring frequently, until the beef is fully cooked; drain.

3. Arrange the tortilla chips in an even layer in the prepared pan. Top with the beef-onion mixture, then top with the beans. Bake, uncovered, for 6 to 8 minutes. Top with the cheese and bake for 5 minutes more, or until the cheese is melted.

4. Drizzle with the salsa. Top as desired with any of the various toppings.

VARIATIONS: Substitute chopped boneless, skinless chicken breasts or fresh Mexican chorizo, casings removed, for the ground beef. Cook in a large skillet and season as directed, then top the tortilla chips with the cooked meat. Proceed as the recipe directs. You can also substitute refried beans, garbanzo beans, or any of your favorite beans for the black beans.

CONVECTION OVEN VARIATION: Prepare the recipe as directed. Bake the beef-and-bean-topped tortilla chips on the Convection Oven setting at 400°F for 5 to 7 minutes. Top with the cheese and bake for 3 to 4 minutes or until the cheese is melted.

Honey Bourbon–Glazed Pork Chops with Sweet Potatoes + Apples

SERVES 2

This is the ideal easy one-pan dinner for a fall evening. Yet why not serve it all summer long, too? Fresh sweet potatoes are now a year-round favorite, and you can make a delicious dinner without heating up the kitchen when using your toaster oven.

1. Preheat the toaster oven to 375°F. Spray a 12 x 12-inch baking pan with nonstick cooking spray.

2. Place the sweet potatoes on one side of the prepared pan. Spray with nonstick cooking spray. Bake, uncovered, for 20 minutes.

3. Meanwhile, stir the bourbon, honey, oil, onion powder, mustard, and thyme in a small bowl. Season with salt and pepper and set aside.

4. Turn the potatoes over. Place the pork chops on the other end of the pan in a single layer. Arrange the apple wedges around the potatoes and pork chops, stacking the apples as needed. Brush the bourbon mixture generously over all. Bake for 15 to 18 minutes or until the pork is done as desired and a meat thermometer registers a minimum of 145°F.

5. For additional browning, set the toaster oven to Broil and broil for 2 to 4 minutes, or until the edges are brown as desired.

6. Transfer to a serving platter. Spoon any drippings over the meat and vegetables. Let stand for 5 minutes before serving.

Nonstick cooking spray

2 medium sweet potatoes, peeled and quartered

2 tablespoons bourbon

2 tablespoons honey

1 tablespoon canola or vegetable oil

½ teaspoon onion powder

½ teaspoon dry mustard

¼ teaspoon dried thyme leaves

Kosher salt and freshly ground black pepper

2 bone-in pork chops, cut about ¾ inch thick

1 Granny Smith apple, not peeled, cored and cut into ½-inch wedges

CONVECTION OVEN VARIATION: Prepare the recipe as directed. Bake the sweet potatoes on the Convection Oven setting at 375°F for 16 to 18 minutes. Turn the potatoes. Add the meat and apples, brush with sauce, and bake for 13 to 15 minutes or until the meat is done as desired and a meat thermometer registers a minimum of 145°F. Turn to broil if additional browning is desired. Proceed as the recipe directs.

CASSEROLES
+
ONE-DISH
DINNERS

Favorite Baked Ziti

SERVES 4 TO 6

2 tablespoons olive oil

1 small onion, diced

3 cloves garlic, minced

¼ teaspoon red pepper flakes

1 pound lean ground beef

½ teaspoon kosher salt

¼ cup dry red wine

1 (14.5-ounce) can crushed tomatoes

1 tablespoon tomato paste

16 ounces ziti, uncooked

Nonstick cooking spray

⅓ cup grated Parmesan cheese

1½ cups shredded mozzarella cheese

2 ounces fresh mozzarella cheese, cut into cubes (about ½ cup)

There is no better meal to prepare for comfort than baked ziti. Roxanne's family loves the crispy, almost burned edges. Serve with garlic bread and Italian salad, and this will become your most requested dinner.

1. Heat the olive oil in a large skillet over medium-high heat. Add the onion and cook, stirring frequently, until tender, 3 to 4 minutes. Stir in the garlic and red pepper flakes. Add the ground beef and salt. Cook, breaking up the ground beef, until the meat is brown and cooked through. Drain well, if needed, and return to the skillet.

2. Add the wine and cook for 2 minutes. Add the tomatoes, tomato paste, and ¾ cup water. Reduce the heat and simmer, uncovered, for 20 to 25 minutes, stirring occasionally.

3. Cook the ziti according to the package directions, except reduce the cooking time to 7 minutes. The ziti will be harder than al dente, which is what you want. Drain and rinse under cold water. Transfer to a large bowl.

4. Preheat the toaster oven to 425°F. Spray an 11 x 7 x 2½-inch baking dish with nonstick cooking spray. Spoon about 1 cup of the meat sauce into the prepared dish. Add half of the ziti in an even layer. Spoon about half of the remaining sauce over the ziti. Sprinkle with half the Parmesan and all the shredded mozzarella. Add the remaining half of ziti and cover with the remaining sauce. Sprinkle the remaining Parmesan on top.

5. Bake, covered, for 20 minutes. Remove from the oven and add the cubes of fresh mozzarella. Bake, uncovered, for an additional 10 minutes. If desired, turn to broil for a few minutes to make the top crispy and brown.

6. Remove from the oven and let stand for 10 minutes before serving.

Nice + Easy Baked Macaroni + Cheese

SERVES 6

Finally! A delicious macaroni and cheese recipe that does not require you to first cook the macaroni and dirty one more pan. By layering the dry macaroni into the casserole and topping with cheese and a milk sauce, this dish is ready to bake in minutes.

1. Preheat the toaster oven to 425°F. Spray an 11 x 7 x 2½-inch baking dish with nonstick cooking spray.

2. Place the milk, cream cheese, salt, garlic, and pepper into a blender. Blend until smooth.

3. Add macaroni to the prepared dish. Sprinkle with the cheddar cheese. Pour the milk mixture over all.

4. Combine the butter, Parmesan, and panko in a small bowl. Sprinkle the crumb mixture over the macaroni. Bake, uncovered, for 25 to 35 minutes or until the top is golden brown. Remove from the oven and let stand for at least 10 minutes.

TIPS: Use any type of cheese that you might have on hand in place of the cheddar cheese.

Do not omit the bread crumb topping on this casserole, as the top of the casserole will overbrown and burn. The crumb topping will bake to a beautiful golden brown.

Nonstick cooking spray

2 cups whole milk

3 ounces cream cheese

½ teaspoon kosher salt

1 clove garlic

¼ teaspoon freshly ground black pepper

8 ounces macaroni, uncooked

2 cups shredded cheddar cheese

2 tablespoons unsalted butter, melted

¼ cup grated Parmesan cheese

1 cup panko bread crumbs

Cheesy Chicken–Stuffed Shells

SERVES 4

Nonstick cooking spray

16 jumbo pasta shells

1 cup finely diced cooked chicken

1 cup whole milk ricotta cheese

1¼ cups shredded mozzarella cheese

1 large egg, slightly beaten

⅓ cup grated Parmesan cheese

1 teaspoon Italian seasoning

2 cloves garlic, minced

¼ teaspoon kosher salt

¼ teaspoon freshly ground black pepper

1½ cups marinara sauce

Baked pasta can come together so quickly and makes a meal that equals delicious comfort. This easy weeknight meal is complete in and of itself. Of course, you can always add a green salad and make this a wonderful ending to a busy day.

1. Preheat the toaster oven to 350°F. Spray an 8 x 8-inch square baking pan with nonstick cooking spray.

2. Cook the shells according to the package directions, drain, and rinse with cool water.

3. Combine the chicken, ricotta, ¾ cup of the mozzarella, egg, Parmesan, Italian seasoning, garlic, salt, and pepper in a large bowl.

4. Spread about ¾ cup of the marinara sauce in the prepared pan. Fill each shell with a heaping tablespoon of the chicken-cheese mixture. Place the prepared shells, stuffed side up, in the pan. Pour the remaining marinara over the shells.

5. Cover and bake for 25 to 30 minutes. Sprinkle with the remaining ½ cup mozzarella and bake, uncovered, for an additional 5 to 10 minutes or until the cheese is melted. Remove from the oven and let stand for 5 to 10 minutes before serving.

VARIATION: This becomes a delicious vegetarian dish if you omit the chicken. Or, for a quick alternative to the 1 cup cooked chicken, use two (4.5-ounce) cans chicken breast, drained and flaked, for the cooked chicken listed in this recipe.

Sage, Chicken + Mushroom Pasta Casserole

SERVES 6

This creamy chicken and pasta casserole gets an up-to-date makeover with the addition of fresh sage and mushrooms.

1. Preheat the toaster oven to 350°F. Spray a 2-quart baking pan with nonstick cooking spray.

2. Cook the pasta according to the package directions; drain and set aside.

3. Melt the butter in a large skillet over medium-high heat. Add the mushrooms and cook, stirring frequently, until the liquid has evaporated, 7 to 10 minutes. Blend in the flour and cook, stirring constantly, for 1 minute. Season with salt and pepper. Gradually stir in the milk and wine. Cook, stirring constantly, until the mixture bubbles and begins to thicken. Remove from the heat. Stir in the sage, cooked pasta, chicken, and fontina. Season with salt and pepper.

4. Spoon into the prepared pan. Cover and bake for 25 to 30 minutes. Uncover, sprinkle with the Parmesan, and bake for an additional 5 minutes or until the cheese is melted.

5. Remove from the oven and let stand for 5 to 10 minutes before serving.

TIPS: If you desire, substitute a 9 x 5-inch loaf pan for the 2-quart baking pan listed in this recipe.

If you prefer, substitute ½ cup chicken broth for the white wine.

Nonstick cooking spray

8 ounces bow-tie pasta, uncooked

4 tablespoons unsalted butter

8 ounces button or white mushrooms, sliced

3 tablespoons all-purpose flour

Kosher salt and freshly ground black pepper

2 cups whole milk

½ cup dry white wine

2 tablespoons minced fresh sage

1½ cups chopped cooked chicken

1 cup shredded fontina, Monterey Jack, or Swiss cheese

½ cup shredded Parmesan cheese

Individual Chicken Pot Pies

SERVES 4

3 tablespoons unsalted butter

½ medium onion, chopped

1 carrot, chopped

1 stalk celery, chopped

1¼ cups sliced button or white mushrooms

2 tablespoons all-purpose flour

1¼ cups whole milk

1 tablespoon fresh lemon juice

½ teaspoon dried thyme leaves

Kosher salt and freshly ground black pepper

1½ cups chopped cooked chicken

½ cup frozen peas

Nonstick cooking spray

1 sheet frozen puff pastry, about 9 inches square, thawed (½ of a 17.3-ounce package)

1 large egg

CONVECTION OVEN SETTING: Prepare the recipe as directed. Bake on the Convection Oven setting at 375°F for 18 to 22 minutes, or until the crust is golden brown.

Can any dish be more soothing and inviting than a chicken pot pie? We doubt it. This delicious pot pie is great freshly made, but for a quick dinner another evening, go ahead and make a batch to freeze. Just fill the ramekins, cover, and stick in the freezer. They'll be ready and waiting to pop into the toaster oven whenever you want an easy dinner.

1. Melt the butter in a large skillet over medium-high heat. Add the onion, carrot, and celery and cook, stirring frequently, for 3 minutes. Add the mushrooms and cook, stirring frequently, for 7 to 10 minutes or until the liquid has evaporated. Blend in the flour and cook, stirring for 1 minute. (Be sure all of the flour is blended into the butter and vegetables.) Gradually stir in the milk. Cook, stirring constantly, until the mixture bubbles and thickens. Stir in the lemon juice and thyme and season with salt and pepper. Stir in the chicken and peas. Remove from the heat and set aside.

2. Preheat the toaster oven to 375°F. Spray 4 (8-ounce) oven-safe ramekins with nonstick cooking spray.

3. Roll the puff pastry out on a lightly floured board, to make an even 10-inch square. Cut the pastry into circles using a 4-inch cutter.

4. Spoon a heaping ¾ cup of filling into each prepared ramekin. Place a puff pastry circle on top of each and crimp the edges to seal to the ramekin. Using the tip of a paring knife, cut 3 slits in each crust to allow steam to escape. Whisk the egg with 1 tablespoon water in a small bowl. Brush the egg mixture over the top of the crust.

5. Bake for 20 to 25 minutes, or until the crust is golden brown. Remove from the oven and let stand for 5 minutes before serving.

TIPS: To freeze the pot pies, prepare the filling as directed and fill the ramekins. Top each with puff pastry circles, crimp the edges, and cut slits in the pastry as directed. Do not brush with the egg. Cover each with aluminum foil. Place in a freezer bag or container, seal, and freeze. When ready to bake, preheat the oven as directed. Do not thaw the pot pies. Leave the pot pies covered with foil and bake at 375F° for 25 minutes. Uncover and brush the top with the egg mixture. Bake, uncovered, for an additional 15 to 20 minutes, or until the filling is hot and the crust is golden.

If desired, cut the scraps of puff pastry into decorative cutouts. It is fun to cut shapes to match the season, the initials for your family, hearts, or any of your favorite shapes. Cut them free form or use a small cookie cutter. Using a small amount of the egg wash as glue, top the pot pies with the decorative cutout before baking. Bake as directed.

Chicken Tortilla Roll-Ups

SERVES 4

Nonstick cooking spray

¼ cup olive oil

2 cloves garlic, minced

1½ cups shredded cooked chicken

1 cup shredded Mexican blend or cheddar cheese

½ cup frozen corn, thawed

⅓ cup salsa verde

1 green onion, white and green portions, chopped

2 tablespoons minced fresh cilantro

1 tablespoon fresh lime juice

½ teaspoon ground cumin

¼ teaspoon Sriracha or hot sauce

Kosher salt and freshly ground black pepper

8 flour tortillas, about 8 inches in diameter

Optional toppings: minced cilantro, salsa, guacamole, sour cream

CONVECTION OVEN SETTING: Prepare the recipe as directed. Bake on the Convection Oven setting at 375°F for 8 to 9 minutes, or until the tortillas are crisp and the filling is hot. Proceed as the recipe directs.

Are you hungry for a crisp flauta, but hate the thought of deep-frying? Then this is the recipe for you. The tortillas bake up crisp, so they are a great handheld snack or easy dinner that everyone, even the kids, will love. This recipe begins with shredded chicken, but shredded beef or pork would also be great. The salsa verde goes especially well with chicken, but if you begin with beef or pork, substitute your favorite red salsa.

1. Preheat the toaster oven to 375°F. Spray a 12 x 12-inch baking pan with nonstick cooking spray.

2. Stir the oil and garlic in a small bowl; set aside.

3. Stir the chicken, cheese, corn, salsa verde, green onion, cilantro, lime juice, cumin, and Sriracha in a large bowl. Season with salt and pepper.

4. Brush both sides of a tortilla very lightly with the garlic oil. Spoon about ⅓ cup chicken filling on the lower side of the tortilla. Roll the tortilla over the filling. Place the filled tortilla, seam side down, in the prepared baking pan. Repeat with the remaining tortillas and filling.

5. Brush the tops of each filled tortilla with the remaining garlic oil, coating them evenly and especially covering the edges of the tortillas.

6. Bake, uncovered, for 10 minutes or until the tortillas are crisp and the filling is hot. Serve with your choice of any of the various toppings.

TIPS: This is a great recipe to substitute leftovers from the roast chicken on page 121. In a pinch, substitute one (12.5-ounce) can chicken breast, drained and flaked, for the 1½ cups chicken in this recipe.

When baking all eight roll-ups in the 12 x 12-inch pan, the tortillas will touch each other. For extra-crisp roll-ups, arrange half of the tortillas in the baking pan, placing them about 1 inch apart and not touching. Bake as directed, then repeat with the remaining roll ups.

Homemade Beef Enchiladas

SERVES 4

Roxanne's family loves Mexican food and frequently dines at Mexican restaurants. That is until she started making enchiladas at home and discovered there's no need to venture out of the house. Now you, too, can enjoy delicious restaurant fare at home.

1. Heat the oil in a small saucepan over medium-high heat. Add the flour and whisk for about a minute. Stir in the chili powder, cumin, garlic powder, and salt. Gradually stir in the broth, whisking until smooth. Reduce the heat to a simmer and cook the sauce for 10 to 12 minutes.

2. Cook the ground beef in a medium skillet over medium-high heat until browned and cooked through, stirring to crumble into a fine texture. Remove from the heat and drain.

3. Preheat the toaster oven to 350°F. Spray an 11 x 7 x 2½-inch baking dish with nonstick cooking spray. Place about ½ cup sauce over the bottom of the dish. Lay a tortilla on a large plate and spread about 2 tablespoons of sauce over the surface of the tortilla. Spoon 2 tablespoons of the ground beef down the center of the tortilla. Sprinkle with some onion and cheese (amount is up to you). Roll up and place in the baking dish. Repeat with the remaining tortillas. Pour the remaining sauce over the top. Sprinkle with remaining cheese. Bake, uncovered, for 20 minutes or until the tortillas are heated through and slightly crisp on the outside.

TIPS: Garnish with chopped fresh cilantro, diced avocado, sour cream, or crumbled cotija cheese, if desired.

VARIATIONS: This makes equally delicious chicken enchiladas. Use roasted chicken pieces in place of the ground beef.

If you like, stir a cup of rinsed and drained pinto, red, or black beans into the ground beef mixture. Reduce the amount of ground beef to ½ pound.

1 tablespoon canola or vegetable oil

1 tablespoon plus 1 teaspoon all-purpose flour

2 tablespoons chili powder

½ teaspoon ground cumin

½ teaspoon garlic powder

¼ teaspoon kosher salt

1¼ cups chicken or vegetable broth

¾ pound lean ground beef

Nonstick cooking spray

8 flour or corn tortillas

¼ cup finely chopped onion

1½ cups shredded Mexican-blend or cheddar cheese

CONVECTION OVEN SETTING: Prepare the recipe as directed. Bake on the Convection Oven setting at 350°F for 16 to 18 minutes, or until the tortillas are cooked through and slightly crisp on the outside.

Couscous-Stuffed Poblano Peppers

SERVES 6

Your grandma may have made stuffed peppers, which may remind you of times gone by, but the wonderful flavor in this recipe is fresh and new. Israeli couscous, a tiny, pearl-shaped pasta that retains its delicious texture and wheat flavor, is combined with the cheese to make a tasty filling for the poblano peppers in this dish. It makes an ideal vegetarian entrée.

1. Heat 1 tablespoon oil in a medium saucepan over medium heat. Add the couscous and cook, stirring frequently, until golden brown, 2 to 3 minutes. Stir in the broth and season with salt and pepper. Cover, reduce the heat to a simmer, and cook, stirring occasionally, for about 10 minutes or until the liquid is absorbed. Remove from the heat and let stand, covered, for 5 minutes. Remove the cover, stir, and set aside to cool.

2. Heat the remaining 1 tablespoon oil in a small saucepan over medium heat. Add the onion, and cook, stirring frequently, for 3 to 5 minutes or until tender. Stir in the garlic and cook for 30 seconds. Stir in the oregano and cumin and season with salt and pepper. Stir in the tomatoes and simmer for 5 minutes.

3. Preheat the toaster oven to 400°F. Spray a 9-inch square baking pan with nonstick cooking spray. Spoon about one-third of the tomato mixture into the prepared pan. Arrange the peppers, cut side up, in the pan.

4. Stir 1 cup of the cheese into the couscous. Spoon the couscous mixture into the peppers, mounding slightly. Spoon the remaining tomato mixture over the peppers. Cover the pan and bake for 30 minutes.

5. Uncover the pan and sprinkle with the remaining cheese. Bake for 5 minutes or until the cheese is melted.

6. Top as desired with any of the various topping choices.

- 2 tablespoons olive oil
- ⅔ cup Israeli couscous
- 1¼ cups vegetable broth or water
- Kosher salt and freshly ground black pepper
- ½ medium onion, chopped
- 2 cloves garlic, minced
- 1 teaspoon dried oregano leaves
- ½ teaspoon ground cumin
- 1 (14.5-ounce) can fire-roasted diced tomatoes, with liquid
- Nonstick cooking spray
- 3 large poblano peppers, halved lengthwise, seeds and stem removed
- 1½ cups shredded Mexican blend, pepper Jack, or sharp cheddar cheese
- Optional toppings: minced fresh cilantro, sliced jalapeño peppers, diced tomatoes, sliced green onions (white and green portions)

MEATS
+
MAINS

Steak with Herbed Butter

Steaks can be delicious placed under the broiler, but why not kick up the flavor a notch with the addition of a fresh herb-garlic-infused butter?

1. Combine the butter, parsley, chives, garlic, and Worcestershire sauce in a small bowl until well blended; set aside.

2. Preheat the toaster oven to broil.

3. Brush the steaks with olive oil and season with salt and pepper. Place the steak on the broiler rack set over the broiler pan. Place the pan in the toaster oven, positioning the steaks about 3 to 4 inches below the heating element. (Depending on your oven and the thickness of the steak, you may need to set the rack to the middle position.) Broil for 6 minutes, turn the steaks over, and broil for an additional 7 minutes. If necessary to reach the desired doneness, turn the steaks over again and broil for an additional 3 minutes or until you reach your desired doneness.

4. Spread the herb butter generously over the steaks. Allow the steaks to stand for 5 to 10 minutes before slicing and serving.

TIP: Steaks cook uniformly and easily if placed at room temperature for 30 to 60 minutes before cooking.

4 tablespoons unsalted butter, softened

1 tablespoon minced flat-leaf (Italian) parsley

1 tablespoon chopped fresh chives

2 cloves garlic, minced

1 teaspoon Worcestershire sauce

2 beef strip steaks, cut about 1½ inches thick

1 tablespoon olive oil

Kosher salt and freshly ground black pepper

Chipotle-Glazed Meat Loaf

1½ pounds lean ground beef

¼ cup finely chopped onion

½ cup crushed tortilla chips

1 teaspoon ground cumin

½ teaspoon chili powder

½ teaspoon garlic powder

½ teaspoon kosher salt

¼ teaspoon freshly ground black pepper

3 tablespoons chopped pickled jalapeños

3 tablespoons chunky salsa

1 large egg

⅓ cup ketchup

3½ teaspoons minced chipotle chilies in adobo sauce

CONVECTION OVEN VARIATION: Prepare the recipe as directed. Bake on the Convection Oven setting at 375°F for 20 to 30 minutes. Spoon off any collected grease, glaze as directed, and bake an additional 20 to 25 minutes, or until a meat thermometer registers 160°F. Proceed as the recipe directs.

Everyday meat loaf can be versatile by changing it up a bit. The crushed tortilla chips combined with the spices and pickled jalapeños make this a meat loaf that will have everyone around the table clamoring for more. Serve it with guacamole, Mexican-style rice, or refried beans.

1. Preheat the toaster oven to 375°F. Line a 12 x 12-inch baking pan with aluminum foil.

2. Combine the ground beef, onion, tortilla chips, cumin, chili powder, garlic powder, salt, pepper, pickled jalapeños, salsa, and egg in a large bowl, stirring until blended well. Shape the meat mixture into a 9 x 5-inch loaf and place on the prepared pan.

3. Bake, uncovered, for 30 minutes. Carefully remove the meat loaf from the oven and spoon off any collected grease from the pan.

4. Place the ketchup in a small bowl and stir in the chipotle chilies in adobo sauce. Spread the ketchup mixture on top of the meat loaf. Continue to bake for an additional 25 to 35 minutes or until a meat thermometer registers 160°F. Let stand for 10 minutes before slicing.

TIPS: You can easily freeze leftover chipotle chilies in adobo sauce. Place a piece of parchment paper on a baking sheet. Spoon out one or two peppers and sauce in small piles on the parchment. Place the baking sheet into the freezer for at least an hour. Lift the chipotle pieces off the parchment and seal in a freezer bag. Store in the freezer for up to 6 months. When ready to use, just take one out of the bag and let thaw.

VARIATION: Feel free to replace the ketchup and chipotle chilies in adobo sauce with ⅓ cup salsa.

Italian Baked Chicken

SERVES 4

The marinade infuses the chicken with Italian flavor. The addition of salami and Parmesan at the end adds just the perfect touch.

1. If the chicken breasts are large and thick, slice each breast in half lengthwise. Place the chicken in a shallow baking dish.

2. Combine the white wine, olive oil, vinegar, lemon juice, Italian seasoning, garlic, salt, and pepper in a small bowl. Pour over the chicken breasts. Cover and refrigerate for 2 to 8 hours, turning the chicken occasionally to coat.

3. Preheat the toaster oven to 375°F.

4. Drain the chicken, discarding the marinade, and place the chicken in an ungreased 12 x 12-inch baking pan. Bake, uncovered, for 20 to 25 minutes or until the chicken is done and a meat thermometer registers 165°F. Place one slice salami (two pieces) on top of each piece of the chicken. Sprinkle the Parmesan evenly over the chicken breasts and broil for 2 to 3 minutes, or until the cheese is melted and starting to brown.

1 pound boneless, skinless chicken breasts

½ cup dry white wine

3 tablespoons olive oil

2 tablespoons white wine vinegar

2 tablespoons fresh lemon juice

2 teaspoons Italian seasoning

3 cloves garlic, minced

½ teaspoon kosher salt

¼ teaspoon freshly ground black pepper

4 slices salami, cut in half

3 tablespoons shredded Parmesan cheese

CONVECTION OVEN VARIATION: Prepare the recipe as directed. Bake on the Convection Oven setting at 375°F for 18 to 23 minutes, or until the chicken is done and a meat thermometer registers 165°F. Top with the salami and cheese and broil as directed.

Chicken Wellington

SERVES 4

2 small (5- to 6-ounce) boneless, skinless chicken breast halves

Kosher salt and freshly ground black pepper

2 teaspoons Italian seasoning

2 tablespoons olive oil

3 tablespoons unsalted butter, softened

3 ounces cream cheese, softened (about ⅓ cup)

¾ cup shredded Monterey Jack cheese

¼ cup grated Parmesan cheese

1 cup frozen (loose-pack) chopped spinach, thawed and squeezed dry

¾ cup chopped canned artichoke hearts, drained

½ teaspoon garlic powder

1 sheet frozen puff pastry, about 9 inches square, thawed (½ of a 17.3-ounce package)

1 large egg, lightly beaten

CONVECTION OVEN VARIATION: Prepare the recipe as directed. Bake on the Convection Oven setting at 425°F for 20 to 25 minutes, or until the pastry is golden brown and crisp and a meat thermometer inserted into the chicken reaches 165°F.

Beef Wellington is such a traditional dish, but this time we use chicken breasts and top each with a cheesy spinach and artichoke topping. What's not to love? Invite friends or family for dinner and enjoy a delicious meal.

1. Preheat the toaster oven to 425° F. Line a 12 x 12-inch baking pan with parchment paper.

2. Cut the chicken breasts in half lengthwise. Season each piece with the salt, pepper, and Italian seasoning. Fold the thinner end under the larger piece to make the chicken breasts into a rounded shape. Secure with toothpicks.

3. Heat a large skillet over medium-high heat. Add the olive oil and heat. Add the chicken breasts and brown well, turning to brown evenly. Remove from the skillet and set aside to cool. Remove the toothpicks.

4. Stir the butter, cream cheese, Monterey Jack, and Parmesan in a large bowl. Stir in the spinach, artichoke hearts, and garlic powder. Season with salt and pepper.

5. Roll out the puff pastry sheet on a lightly floured board until it makes a 12-inch square. Cut into four equal pieces. Spread one-fourth of the spinach-artichoke mixture on the surface of each pastry square to within ½ inch of all four edges. Place the chicken in the center of each. Gently fold the puff pastry up over the chicken and pinch the edges to seal tightly.

6. Place each chicken bundle, seam side down, on the prepared pan. Brush the top of each bundle lightly with the beaten egg. Bake for 25 to 30 minutes, or until the pastry is golden brown and crisp and a meat thermometer inserted into the chicken reaches 165°F.

TIP: To make ahead, assemble as directed, then freeze. Seal tightly in a freezer container and label. When ready to prepare, place the frozen bundles on the baking sheet. Bake as directed, increasing the baking time to 45 minutes.

Roast Chicken

SERVES 6

No need to stop and pick up a rotisserie-style chicken at the grocery store. This recipe is big on flavor, yet easy to put in the toaster oven, and you can let it roast to perfection while you are busy with other tasks. No basting. No fussing. No stress.

1. Preheat the toaster oven to 350°F. Spray a 12 x 12-inch baking pan with nonstick cooking spray.

2. Drizzle the chicken cavity with about half of the lemon juice. Place half of the juiced lemon into the chicken cavity. Truss the chicken using kitchen twine.

3. Rub the chicken evenly with the olive oil.

4. Stir the salt, garlic powder, lemon zest, thyme, and pepper in a small bowl. Using your fingertips, rub the seasonings evenly over the chicken. Place the chicken, breast side up, in the prepared pan. Drizzle with the remaining lemon juice.

5. Roast, uncovered, for 1¼ hours to 1½ hours, or until a meat thermometer registers 165°F. Let stand for 10 minutes before carving.

TIP: To truss a chicken means to tie the chicken legs and wings close to the body of the chicken using kitchen or cooking twine so that the chicken holds a compact shape as it cooks.

Nonstick cooking spray

1 whole (3½ -pound) chicken

Grated zest and juice of 1 lemon

1 tablespoon olive oil

1½ teaspoons kosher salt

1 teaspoon garlic powder

½ teaspoon dried thyme leaves

½ teaspoon freshly ground black pepper

CONVECTION OVEN VARIATION: Prepare the recipe as directed. Roast on the Convection Oven setting at 350°F for 1 hour to 1¼ hours or until a meat thermometer registers 165°F. Proceed as the recipe directs.

Crispy Chicken Tenders

1 pound boneless, skinless chicken breasts

½ cup all-purpose flour

½ teaspoon kosher salt

¼ teaspoon freshly ground black ground pepper

1 large egg, beaten

3 tablespoons whole milk

1 cup cornflake crumbs

½ cup grated Parmesan cheese

Nonstick cooking spray

CONVECTION OVEN VARIATION: Prepare the recipe as directed. Bake on the Convection Oven setting at 375°F for 9 minutes. Turn the chicken and spray with nonstick cooking spray. Bake for an additional 8 to 10 minutes, or until the chicken is crisp and a meat thermometer registers 165°F.

You can feel great about serving these to your family, as they are much better than the processed and frozen alternative available at the supermarket. Serve these with ranch dressing for the kids and buffalo sauce for adults.

1. Preheat the toaster oven to 375°F. Line a 12 x 12-inch baking pan with nonstick aluminum foil. (Or if lining the pan with regular foil, spray it with nonstick cooking spray.)

2. Cover the chicken with plastic wrap. Pound the chicken with the flat side of a meat pounder until it is even and about ½ inch thick. Cut the chicken into strips about 1 by 3 inches.

3. Combine the flour, salt, and pepper in a small shallow dish. Place the egg and milk in another small shallow dish and use a fork to combine. Place the cornflake crumbs and Parmesan in a third small shallow dish and combine.

4. Dredge each chicken piece in the flour, then dip in the egg mixture, and then coat with the cornflake crumb mixture. Place the chicken strips in a single layer in the prepared baking pan. Spray the chicken strips generously with nonstick cooking spray.

5. Bake for 10 minutes. Turn the chicken and spray with nonstick cooking spray. Bake for an additional 10 to 12 minutes, or until crisp and a meat thermometer registers 165°F.

TIP: About 3 cups of cornflakes will make the 1 cup of crumbs. You can quickly and easily make the crumbs by processing the cornflakes in a food processor. Or, place the cereal in a zip-top bag and crush until it forms fine and even crumbs.

VARIATION: For a change of flavor, substitute 1 cup of finely crushed pretzels for the cornflake crumbs. Process the pretzels in a food processor until they form fine and even crumbs.

Tuscan Pork Tenderloin

SERVES 4

So elegant and yet so very simple to prepare, this pork tenderloin is stuffed with basil, prosciutto, and mozzarella. Pork is a very lean cut, so watch the cooking process carefully and do not overcook.

1. Preheat the toaster oven to 400°F. Spray a 12 x 12-inch baking pan with nonstick cooking spray.

2. Cut the pork tenderloin in half lengthwise, not quite cutting through one side, and gently open it (like a book) so it lays flat. Cover the meat with plastic wrap. Pound the meat with the flat side of a meat pounder until the meat is even and about ½ inch thick.

3. Season the cut side of the meat with salt and pepper. Arrange the basil leaves evenly over the meat, then sprinkle with 1 teaspoon of the minced garlic. Top with an even layer of prosciutto and cheese. Roll the meat from the longer side covering the cheese and other filling ingredients completely. Tie the meat shut with kitchen twine, taking care to keep the roll tight and the filling inside.

4. Rub the outside of the meat with the olive oil. Mix the Italian seasoning and the remaining ½ teaspoon garlic in a small bowl. Season with salt and pepper. Rub the seasoning mixture evenly over the meat.

5. Place the meat in the prepared pan. Roast, uncovered, for 25 to 35 minutes or until the tenderloin is brown and the pork is just slightly pink inside.

6. Let stand for 5 to 10 minutes. Slice crosswise into slices about 1 inch thick.

Nonstick cooking spray.

1 pork tenderloin (1¼ to 1½ pounds)

Kosher salt and freshly ground black pepper

8 to 10 fresh basil leaves

1½ teaspoons minced garlic (about 3 cloves garlic)

2 slices prosciutto

2 ounces mozzarella cheese, cut into thin strips, or ½ cup shredded

1 tablespoon olive oil

1 teaspoon Italian seasoning

CONVECTION OVEN VARIATION: Prepare the recipe as directed. Roast on the Convection Oven setting at 400°F for 20 to 30 minutes, or until brown and the meat is just slightly pink inside. Proceed as the recipe directs.

Spanish Pork Skewers

SERVES 4

1 pound pork tenderloin, cut into ¾- to 1-inch cubes

2 tablespoons olive oil

1 teaspoon ground cumin

½ teaspoon smoked paprika

½ teaspoon dried thyme leaves

½ teaspoon kosher salt, plus more for seasoning

⅛ teaspoon red pepper flakes

2 cloves garlic, minced

1 red bell pepper, cut into ¾- to 1-inch squares

1 small red onion, cut into ¾- to 1-inch wedges

Freshly ground black pepper

Nonstick cooking spray

2 tablespoons unsalted butter

1 tablespoon sherry or balsamic vinegar

1 teaspoon packed dark brown sugar

These skewers, inspired by the flavors of Spain, are richly flavored but are not spicy hot. The tender pork cubes, red bell peppers, and onions are flavored with garlic, smoked paprika, cumin, and olive oil, while sherry vinegar adds a tangy flavor to the glaze. They're a great change of pace for dinner, but also make delicious appetizers or tapas when you thread the pork and vegetables onto 4-inch skewers.

1. Place the pork cubes in a medium bowl. Drizzle 1 tablespoon of oil over the pork. Stir the cumin, paprika, thyme, ½ teaspoon salt, the pepper flakes, and garlic in a small bowl. Sprinkle the seasonings over the pork. Stir to coat the pork evenly. Cover and refrigerate for at least 4 hours or up to overnight.

2. Place the bell pepper and onion pieces in a medium bowl. Drizzle with the remaining tablespoon olive oil and season with salt and pepper. Toss to coat evenly.

3. Alternately thread the pork and vegetables onto skewers. Spray a 12 x 12-inch baking pan with nonstick cooking spray. Place the filled skewers on the prepared pan. Place the pan in the toaster oven, positioning the skewers about 3 to 4 inches below the heating element. (Depending on your oven, you may need to set the rack to the middle position.)

4. Set the toaster oven on broil. Broil for 10 minutes. Turn the skewers. Broil for an additional 5 minutes, or until the vegetables are tender and a meat thermometer registers 145°F. Do not overcook.

5. Meanwhile, combine the butter, vinegar, and brown sugar in a small, glass, microwave-safe bowl. Season with salt and pepper. Microwave on High (100 percent) power for 45 seconds or until the butter melts and the mixture begins to bubble. Stir to dissolve the sugar.

6. Lightly brush the vinegar mixture over the skewers. Broil for 1 minute or until the skewers are browned.

TIPS: Select skewers that fit comfortably inside your toaster oven and on the baking pan. If you are using bamboo skewers, which are available in a variety of lengths, soak the skewers in cold water for 30 minutes before cooking.

The pork and vegetables are equally delicious baked on a baking pan without threading onto skewers.

Roasted Garlic Shrimp

SERVES 4

Roast shrimp in just moments in your toaster oven. This delectable garlic, herb, and lemon flavor will remind you of a restaurant meal. For dinner, hot cooked rice or pasta completes the meal. These shrimp also make a tantalizing appetizer. They are so good, we bet you won't have leftovers, but if you do, they are tasty tossed in a pasta salad or served on a bed of salad greens.

1. Preheat the toaster oven to 400°F. Spray a 12 x 12-inch baking pan with nonstick cooking spray.

2. Mix the melted butter, garlic, lemon zest, thyme, and pepper in a small bowl. Season with salt. Set aside.

3. Arrange the shrimp in a single layer in the prepared pan. Pour the butter mixture over the shrimp, then stir gently to coat the shrimp.

4. Roast, uncovered, for 10 to 12 minutes or until the shrimp turn pink. Drizzle with the lemon juice. Transfer to a serving platter and spoon any collected drippings over the shrimp. Garnish, if desired, with minced parsley.

Nonstick cooking spray

¼ cup unsalted butter, melted

2 cloves garlic, minced

1 teaspoon grated lemon zest

½ teaspoon dried thyme leaves

¼ teaspoon freshly ground black pepper

Kosher salt

1 pound uncooked large shrimp, fresh or frozen and thawed, peeled and deveined

1½ tablespoons fresh lemon juice

Optional: Minced fresh flat-leaf (Italian) parsley

CONVECTION OVEN VARIATION: Prepare the recipe as directed. Roast on the Convection Oven setting at 400°F for 8 to 10 minutes or until the shrimp turn pick. Proceed as the recipe directs.

Lemon-Roasted Fish with Olives + Capers

SERVES 4

Nonstick cooking spray

1 pound cod or white-fleshed, mild-flavored fillets, patted dry

Kosher salt and freshly ground black pepper

½ teaspoon paprika

1 large lemon

3 tablespoons dry white wine

½ cup pitted kalamata or other variety olives, drained

2 tablespoons capers, drained

1 tablespoon olive oil

CONVECTION OVEN VARIATION: Prepare the recipe as directed. Roast on the Convection Oven setting at 425°F for 8 to 9 minutes, or until the fish flakes easily with a fork and a meat thermometer registers 145°F. Proceed as the recipe directs.

The olives and capers add a slight but unmistakable tart and salty flavor to this mild-flavored fish. If your grocery store has an olive bar, this is the perfect time to choose your favorite olives or mix and match for a new flavor twist.

1. Preheat the toaster oven to 425°F. Spray a 12 x 12-inch baking pan with nonstick cooking spray.

2. Place the fish fillets on the prepared pan. Season with salt, pepper, and paprika.

3. Slice the lemon in half. Slice one half crosswise into almost paper-thin slices. Arrange the slices evenly over the fish. Juice the remaining half of the lemon and drizzle over the fish. Drizzle the wine over the fish. Top with the olives and capers, then drizzle with the olive oil.

4. Roast for 10 minutes or until the fish flakes easily with a fork and a meat thermometer registers 145°F. To serve, spoon the pan drippings, olives, and capers over the fish.

Roasted Fish with Provençal Crumb Topping

SERVES 3

Even the pickiest family member will be asking you to prepare this recipe again and again. The toasted, seasoned bread crumbs add a flavorful accent everyone loves. You can use any firm-textured white fish.

1. Preheat the toaster oven to 400°F. Lightly grease the baking pan with olive oil.

2. Heat the tablespoon of olive oil in a small skillet over medium-high heat. Add the onion and cook, stirring frequently, for 3 to 4 minutes, or until tender. Add the garlic and cook for 30 seconds. Remove the skillet from the heat. Stir in the bread crumbs, parsley, and thyme.

3. Place the fish in the prepared pan. Drizzle with the wine. Divide the crumb mixture evenly over the top of each fish fillet, and press onto the fillets. Roast for 20 to 25 minutes, or until the top is brown and the fish is opaque and flakes easily when tested with a fork. Sprinkle the lemon juice evenly over the fish.

TIP: If you do not have fresh bread crumbs available, you can substitute panko bread crumbs.

1 tablespoon olive oil, plus more for greasing

⅓ cup finely chopped onion

1 clove garlic, minced

¾ cup fresh bread crumbs

2 tablespoons chopped fresh flat-leaf (Italian) parsley

1 teaspoon fresh thyme leaves

3 (5-ounce) cod fillets, or other white-fleshed, mild-flavored fish, patted dry (about 1¼ inches thick)

2 tablespoons dry white wine

2 teaspoons fresh lemon juice

CONVECTION OVEN VARIATION: Prepare the recipe as directed. Roast on the Convection Oven setting at 400°F for 18 to 23 minutes or until the fish flakes easily. Proceed as the recipe directs.

10

DESSERTS

German Chocolate Cake

SERVES 6

Butter, shortening, or nonstick cooking spray

⅔ cup whole milk

½ teaspoon white vinegar

⅔ cup all-purpose flour

3 tablespoons unsweetened cocoa powder

½ teaspoon baking soda

½ teaspoon baking powder

¼ teaspoon table salt

½ cup packed dark brown sugar

2 tablespoons canola or vegetable oil

1 large egg

½ teaspoon pure vanilla extract

GERMAN CHOCOLATE FROSTING

1 large egg yolk

½ cup evaporated milk

⅓ cup granulated sugar

3 tablespoons unsalted butter

¾ cup sweetened flaked coconut

⅓ cup chopped pecans, toasted

German chocolate cake is a favorite for birthdays and other special occasions. This recipe is perfectly sized to enjoy a single-layer cake and, of course, the best part is the creamy, nutty, coconut-filled frosting on top.

1. Preheat the toaster oven to 350°F. Line an 8-inch round cake pan with parchment paper and lightly grease the bottom and sides with butter or shortening or spray with nonstick cooking spray.

2. Pour the milk into a medium bowl and stir in the vinegar; set aside.

3. Whisk the flour, cocoa, baking soda, baking powder, and salt in a small bowl; set aside.

4. Whisk the brown sugar, oil, egg, and vanilla in a medium bowl. Add the flour mixture, in thirds, alternately with the milk mixture, beginning and ending with the flour. Blend well and scrape the sides of the bowl as needed.

5. Pour the batter into the prepared pan. Bake for 20 to 25 minutes, or until a wooden pick inserted into the center comes out clean. Let cool on a wire rack for 10 minutes. Invert onto a serving platter and allow to cool completely.

6. Make the frosting: Combine the egg yolk, evaporated milk, sugar, and butter in a small saucepan. Cook, stirring, over medium heat for about 6 minutes or until thickened and bubbly. Remove from the heat and stir in the coconut and pecans. Cover and let cool completely. Frost the top of the cake.

Chocolate Caramel Pecan Cupcakes

MAKES 6

6 tablespoons all-purpose flour

6 tablespoons unsweetened cocoa powder

¼ teaspoon baking soda

¼ teaspoon baking powder

⅛ teaspoon table salt

6 tablespoons unsalted butter, softened

½ cup granulated sugar

1 large egg

½ teaspoon pure vanilla extract

½ cup sour cream

BUTTERCREAM FROSTING

¼ cup unsalted butter, softened

1¾ cups confectioners' sugar

2 to 3 tablespoons half-and-half or milk

1 teaspoon pure vanilla extract

Caramel ice cream topping

¼ cup caramelized chopped pecans (see tips)

CONVECTION OVEN VARIATION: Prepare the recipe as directed. Bake on the Convection Oven setting at 350°F for 16 to 18 minutes, or until a wooden pick inserted into the center comes out clean. Proceed as the recipe directs.

It's party time, and these cupcakes will help you celebrate all of life's milestones. And another reason to celebrate is that you won't have leftovers. This unbeatable recipe makes just six of the best chocolate cupcakes you can imagine. Then you frost the cupcakes with buttercream frosting, a drizzle of caramel, and for a finishing touch, caramelized pecans.

1. Preheat the toaster oven to 350°F. Line a 6-cup muffin pan with cupcake papers.

2. Whisk the flour, cocoa, baking soda, baking powder, and salt in a small bowl; set aside.

3. Beat the butter and granulated sugar in a large bowl with a handheld mixer at medium-high speed for 2 minutes, or until the mixture is light and creamy. Beat in the egg well. Beat in the vanilla.

4. On low speed, beat in the flour mixture in thirds, alternating with the sour cream, beginning and ending with the flour mixture. The batter will be thick.

5. Spoon the batter evenly into the prepared cupcake cups, filling each about three-quarters full. Bake for 18 to 20 minutes, or until a wooden pick inserted into the center comes out clean. Place on a wire rack and let cool completely.

6. Meanwhile, make the frosting: Beat the butter in a large bowl using a handheld mixer on medium-high speed until creamy. Gradually beat in the confectioners' sugar. Beat in 2 tablespoons of half-and-half and the vanilla. Beat in the remaining tablespoon of half-and-half, as needed, until the frosting is of desired consistency.

7. Frost each cooled cupcake. Drizzle the caramel topping in thin, decorative stripes over the frosting. Top with the caramelized pecans.

TIPS: Caramelized or glazed chopped pecans are often shelved in the grocery store with salad toppings or snacks. To make your own, melt 1 tablespoon unsalted butter in a small skillet. Stir in 2 tablespoons brown sugar and cook, over medium heat, for 1 minute or until the sugar is melted and just beginning to bubble. Stir in ¼ cup chopped pecans and a dash of ground cinnamon. Cook, stirring constantly, to coat the pecans for 30 seconds. Pour onto a parchment paper–lined baking sheet and let cool completely.

Toasting nuts intensifies their flavor and is easy to do in your toaster oven. See page 21.

Fresh Strawberry Bars

MAKES 16

We are lucky enough to have a plethora of strawberry fields by our homes. When strawberry season arrives, we're the first in line to pick berries—upward of twenty pounds. After making jam, we get busy with other strawberry recipes. This is one of our all-time favorites. Cut these butter-filled, sweet bars into smaller pieces, as they are a rich treat.

1. Preheat the toaster oven to 375°F. Line an 8-inch square pan with nonstick aluminum foil.

2. Beat the butter, flour, salt, and 1 cup of the sugar in a large bowl with a handheld mixer at medium speed, until the mixture is combined and resembles crumbles. Place half of the mixture in the prepared pan. Press down evenly to form a crust.

3. Combine the remaining ⅓ cup sugar, the strawberries, lemon juice, and cornstarch in a medium bowl. Spread evenly over the crust. Sprinkle the remaining crumb mixture over the strawberries. Bake for 50 to 55 minutes or until bubbly and light brown. Let cool completely on a wire rack. They are best served at room temperature.

TIP: These can be frozen up to a month. Thaw to room temperature before serving.

1 cup unsalted butter, softened

2 cups all-purpose flour

½ teaspoon table salt

1⅓ cups sugar

2½ cups sliced fresh strawberries

2 teaspoons fresh lemon juice

2 tablespoons cornstarch

CONVECTION OVEN VARIATION: Prepare the recipe as directed. Bake on the Convection Oven setting at 375°F for 45 to 50 minutes or until bubbly and light brown. Proceed as the recipe directs.

Mississippi Mud Brownies

MAKES 16

An easy one-bowl brownie with a decadent marshmallow filling makes this treat perfect for your family, or quickly bake a batch for a friend in need.

1. Preheat the toaster oven to 350°F. Spray an 8-inch square baking pan with nonstick cooking spray.

2. Beat the cocoa and oil in a large bowl with a handheld mixer at medium speed. Add the butter and mix until smooth. Beat in the granulated sugar. Add the eggs, one at a time, mixing after each addition. Add the vanilla and mix. On low speed, blend in the flour and salt. Stir in the pecans.

3. Pour the batter into the prepared pan. Bake for 28 to 32 minutes, or until a wooden pick inserted into the center comes out clean.

4. Remove the brownies from the oven and sprinkle the marshmallows over the top. Return to the oven and bake for about 2 minutes or until the marshmallows are puffed. Place on a wire rack and let cool completely.

5. Meanwhile, make the frosting: Combine the butter, cocoa, vanilla, confectioners' sugar, and 2 tablespoons milk in a large bowl. Beat until smooth. If needed for the desired consistency, add additional milk. Frost the cooled brownies.

TIP: Does someone in your family dislike nuts? You can easily omit the nuts, or to appeal to everyone, sprinkle ¼ cup nuts over half of the frosted brownies. Everyone wins!

Nonstick cooking spray

3 tablespoons unsweetened cocoa powder

¼ cup canola or vegetable oil

¼ cup unsalted butter, softened

1 cup granulated sugar

2 large eggs

1 teaspoon pure vanilla extract

¾ cup all-purpose flour

½ teaspoon table salt

½ cup pecan pieces, toasted

2 cups mini marshmallows

FROSTING

¼ cup unsalted butter, melted

3 tablespoons unsweetened cocoa powder

½ teaspoon pure vanilla extract

2 cups confectioners' sugar

2 to 3 tablespoons whole milk

CONVECTION OVEN VARIATION: Prepare the recipe as directed. Bake on the Convection Oven setting at 350°F for 25 to 30 minutes, or until a wooden pick inserted into the center comes out clean. Top with the marshmallows and bake for 1 to 2 minutes or until the marshmallows are puffed. Proceed as the recipe directs.

Freezer-to-Oven Chocolate Chip Cookies

MAKES ABOUT 3 DOZEN

2½ cups all-purpose flour

1 teaspoon baking soda

½ teaspoon table salt

¼ teaspoon baking powder

1 cup unsalted butter, softened

1 cup packed dark brown sugar

¾ cup granulated sugar

2 large eggs

2 teaspoons pure vanilla extract

1 (12-ounce) package semisweet chocolate chips

CONVECTION OVEN SETTING: Prepare the recipe as directed. Bake on the Convection Oven setting at 350°F for 11 to 13 minutes or until golden brown. Proceed as the recipe directs.

Can anything beat a warm direct-from-the-oven cookie? For this recipe, make the dough, then bake the cookies now or freeze for baking later. Warm cookies are ready at a moment's notice when sweet snack cravings strike.

1. Preheat the toaster oven to 375°F. Line a 12 x 12-inch baking sheet with parchment paper.

2. Whisk the flour, baking soda, salt, and baking powder in a medium bowl; set aside.

3. Beat the butter, brown sugar, and granulated sugar in a large bowl with a handheld mixer at medium-high speed for 2 minutes or until creamy. Beat in the eggs, one at a time, beating well after each addition. Beat in the vanilla. Mix in the dry ingredients until blended. Stir in the chocolate chips.

4. Using a 2-tablespoon scoop, shape the batter into balls about 1½ inches in diameter. Arrange the cookies 1 inch apart on the prepared baking sheet. Bake for 13 to 15 minutes or until golden brown. Remove from the oven and let cool for 1 minute, then transfer the cookies to a wire rack.

TIP: To freeze, arrange the balls of cookie dough on a parchment paper–lined baking sheet, placing the balls about ½ inch apart. Cover the cookies loosely with plastic wrap. Freeze the cookies for about 1 to 2 hours or until firm. Transfer the cookies to a plastic food bag or freezer container. Seal, label, and date; they can be kept for up to 3 months. Bake as directed for 14 to 16 minutes.

Glazed Apple Crostata

SERVES 6

A crostata is a delicious, rustic, one-crust pie and is easy to make. Place the crust on a baking pan, fill, and fold the edges up over the fruit. The casual look is part of its charm.

1. Place the flour, sugar, and salt in the work bowl of a food processor. Pulse to combine. Add the butter and pulse until it forms coarse crumbs. With the motor running, drizzle in enough cold water that the mixture comes together and forms a dough. Shape the dough into a disk, wrap in plastic wrap, and refrigerate for at least 1 hour or until chilled.

2. Make the filling: Stir the sugar, flour, cinnamon, nutmeg, and salt in a large bowl. Add the apples and stir to coat; set aside.

3. Preheat the toaster oven to 400°F. Line a 12-inch pizza pan or 12 x 12-inch baking pan with parchment paper.

4. Roll the pastry into a 12-inch circle on a lightly floured board. Gently fold the dough into quarters and transfer to the prepared pan. Unfold the dough. Pile the filling in the center of the pastry, leaving a 1- to 2-inch border around the edges. Dot the apples with the butter. Fold the edges of the crust up around the outer edge of the apples. Whisk the egg in a small bowl, then brush the edges of the crust with the egg. Sprinkle the crust with coarse sugar.

5. Bake for 30 to 35 minutes or until golden brown and the apples are tender.

6. Set on a wire rack. For the glaze, microwave the preserves in a small, microwave-safe glass bowl on High (100 percent) power for 30 seconds or until melted. Pour the preserves through a fine mesh strainer. Brush the warm preserves over the apples (but not over the crust). Serve warm.

TIP: If you would rather not make a pastry crust, substitute a prepared refrigerated crust for this recipe.

PASTRY

1¼ cups all-purpose flour

3 tablespoons granulated sugar

¼ teaspoon table salt

½ cup unsalted butter, cut into 1-inch pieces

2½ to 3½ tablespoons ice water

FILLING

¼ cup granulated sugar

3 tablespoons all-purpose flour

½ teaspoon ground cinnamon

¼ teaspoon ground nutmeg

Dash table salt

3 large Granny Smith apples, peeled, cored, and thinly sliced

1 tablespoon unsalted butter, cut into small pieces

1 large egg

Coarse white sugar

GLAZE

¼ cup apricot preserves or apple jelly

CONVECTION OVEN SETTING: Prepare the recipe as directed. Bake on the Convection Oven setting at 400°F for 25 to 30 minutes or until golden brown and the apples are tender. Proceed as the recipe directs.

Easy Peach Turnovers

MAKES 6

1½ tablespoons granulated sugar

1 teaspoon cornstarch

¾ cup chopped peeled peaches, fresh or frozen and thawed

½ teaspoon grated lemon zest

⅛ teaspoon ground nutmeg

Dash table salt

1 sheet frozen puff pastry, about 9 inches square, thawed (½ of a 17.3-ounce package)

1 large egg

Coarse white sugar

GLAZE

¾ cup confectioners' sugar

½ teaspoon pure vanilla extract

1 to 2 tablespoons milk

CONVECTION OVEN VARIATION: Prepare the recipe as directed. Bake on the Convection Oven setting at 375°F for 13 to 18 minutes or until golden brown. Proceed as the recipe directs.

Frozen puff pastry sheets and frozen peach slices combine to make a tasty dessert all year long. We love the fact that you can assemble these, keep them frozen, and bake just the number you want to serve. These tasty turnovers are delicious served warm with a drizzle of glaze. They are also an ideal picnic food—just omit the glaze, wrap loosely in a clean towel, and place in the picnic basket.

1. Line a 12 x 12-inch baking pan with parchment paper.

2. Stir the granulated sugar and cornstarch in a medium bowl. Stir in the peaches, lemon zest, nutmeg, and salt. Mix until the sugar-cornstarch mixture coats the peaches evenly and the sugar begins to dissolve; set aside.

3. On a lightly floured board, roll the puff pastry sheet into a 13½ x 9-inch rectangle. Cut the puff pastry into 6 (4½-inch) squares. Lightly beat the egg in a small bowl, then brush the edges of each puff pastry square with the egg. Reserve the remaining egg to brush on top of each turnover.

4. Spoon about 2 tablespoons peach mixture into the center of each square. Fold the pastry over the peaches to form a triangle, pinching to seal the edges. Using the tines of a fork, crimp the edges tightly. Lightly brush the top of each turnover with the egg. Sprinkle each with the coarse sugar.

5. Place the turnovers on the prepared pan. Freeze the turnovers for 15 minutes.

6. Preheat the toaster oven to 375°F. Bake for 15 to 20 minutes or until golden brown. Let cool 5 to 10 minutes.

7. Meanwhile make the glaze: Whisk the confectioners' sugar, vanilla, and 1 tablespoon milk in a small bowl until smooth. If needed, stir in the additional milk to reach the desired consistency. Drizzle the glaze from the tip of a teaspoon in decorative stripes over the turnovers.

TIPS: If desired, instead of freezing the turnover for 15 minutes, freeze until firm. Once the turnovers are frozen, transfer to a zip-top freezer bag or container and freeze for up to 1 month. When ready to bake, refrigerate for about 3 to 4 hours to partially thaw. Bake and then glaze as directed.

Freezing the shaped turnovers before baking for just 15 minutes means the butter in the puff pastry is chilled and firm. This helps the pastry hold its shape when baking.

Not Key Lime, Lime Pie

MAKES 1 (9-INCH) PIE

We can't find key limes in our local grocery stores very often, but we still want to enjoy this tangy, cool, and refreshing dessert. No worries if you can't either, you can make our version using regular limes. We enjoy it made with all lime juice, but if you want a lighter, less tart flavor, substitute fresh lemon juice for half of the lime juice listed in the recipe. Either way, you can enjoy a slice of lime pie and imagine the bright sunshine of Florida, regardless of where you are.

1. Preheat the toaster oven to 350°F.

2. Whisk the lime zest and egg yolks in a large bowl for 1 minute. Whisk in the sweetened condensed milk and lime juice. Set aside to thicken while you prepare the crust.

3. Stir the graham cracker crumbs, granulated sugar, and salt in a medium bowl. Pour the butter over the mixture and mix until combined and moist. Press the crust evenly into the bottom and up the sides of a 9-inch pie plate. Pack tightly using the back of a large spoon. Bake for 10 minutes. Let cool on a cooling rack.

4. When the crust is completely cool, pour the lime filling inside. Bake for 15 to 17 minutes, or until the center is set (it will still jiggle a bit). Allow the pie to cool completely at room temperature. Spray plastic wrap with nonstick cooking spray and place on the pie. Refrigerate for at least 3 hours or overnight.

5. Beat the cream in a large bowl with an electric mixer at medium-high speed until soft peaks form. Add the confectioners' sugar, one tablespoon at a time, and continue to beat until stiff peaks form. Dollop, pipe, or spread the whipped cream over the pie before serving. Refrigerate leftovers for up to 3 days.

1 tablespoon grated lime zest

3 large egg yolks

1 (14-ounce) can sweetened condensed milk

½ cup fresh lime juice

1¾ cups graham cracker crumbs (about 12 full graham crackers)

⅓ cup granulated sugar

⅛ teaspoon table salt

½ cup unsalted butter, melted

Nonstick cooking spray

WHIPPED CREAM

1 cup heavy cream

⅓ cup confectioners' sugar

Almond Amaretto Bundt Cake

MAKES 1 (12-INCH) CAKE

Nonstick baking spray with flour

1 (15.25- to 18-ounce) box yellow cake mix

1 (3.9-ounce) box vanilla instant pudding

1 cup sour cream

½ cup canola or vegetable oil

¼ cup amaretto or almond liqueur

4 large eggs

¼ teaspoon pure almond extract

GLAZE

2½ cups confectioners' sugar

2 tablespoons amaretto

1 teaspoon pure vanilla extract

1 to 2 tablespoons milk

Sliced almonds, toasted

We wrote an entire cookbook with delicious recipes using the fluted tube pan we all know as a Bundt pan, and still love those cakes for their beauty and flavor. This delicious Bundt cake has a mild, but distinctive, flavor from the amaretto, an almond-flavored liqueur. Both this cake, and the lemon variation, are wonderful served with fresh berries.

1. Preheat the toaster oven to 350°F. Spray a 12-cup Bundt pan with nonstick baking spray with flour.

2. Beat the cake mix, instant pudding, sour cream, oil, ¼ cup water, the amaretto, eggs, and almond extract in a large bowl with a handheld mixer at low speed for 30 seconds to combine the ingredients. Scrape the sides of the bowl with a rubber scraper. Beat on medium-high speed for 2 minutes.

3. Pour the batter into the prepared pan. Bake for 30 to 35 minutes, or until a wooden pick inserted into the center comes out clean.

4. Place the pan on a wire rack to cool for 10 minutes. Invert the cake onto the rack and let cool completely.

5. Meanwhile, make the glaze: Whisk the sugar, amaretto, vanilla, and 1 tablespoon milk in a small bowl. If needed, stir in the additional milk to make the desired consistency. Pour over the cake. Garnish with the sliced almonds.

VARIATION: For a delicious lemon cake, substitute fresh lemon juice for the amaretto. Stir in the grated zest of 1 lemon. Omit the almond extract and add ½ teaspoon lemon extract. Prepare and bake the cake as directed. For the glaze, substitute fresh lemon juice for the amaretto and lemon extract for the vanilla extract. Omit the almond slices. If desired, garnish with fresh berries.

BREADS

Best-Ever Cinnamon Rolls

MAKES 10

1 tablespoon unsalted butter, softened

DOUGH

½ cup whole milk

2 tablespoons unsalted butter, softened

3 tablespoons granulated sugar

½ teaspoon table salt

1 large egg

1⅔ cups all-purpose flour, plus more for kneading and dusting

1¼ teaspoons instant yeast

FILLING

⅔ cup packed dark brown sugar

1 tablespoon plus 1 teaspoon ground cinnamon

Pinch table salt

3 tablespoons unsalted butter, melted

GLAZE

1½ cups confectioners' sugar

1 to 2 tablespoon whole milk

1 tablespoon brewed coffee

½ teaspoon pure vanilla extract

1 tablespoon unsalted butter, melted

These cinnamon rolls will become a weekend morning go-to. The dough is easy to combine and produces a tender, feathery crumb. The best part is that it makes ten rolls, enough to enjoy without leftovers that dry out. Don't forget to brew the coffee, too.

1. Spread the 1 tablespoon softened butter generously on the sides and bottom of an 8-inch round baking pan.

2. Combine the milk, 2 tablespoons softened butter, sugar, and salt in a 4-cup glass measuring cup. Microwave on High (100 percent) power for 40 seconds or until warm (110°F). (All the butter may not melt.) Whisk in the egg.

3. Stir the flour and yeast in a large bowl. Add the liquid ingredients and stir until you have a soft dough. Flour your hands and a clean surface. Transfer the dough to the floured surface and form it into a ball. Add flour as necessary and knead by pressing the dough with the heel of your hands and turning and repeating. Add just enough flour to keep the dough from being sticky.

4. When the dough is smooth and springs back when you press it with you finger (after 3 to 5 minutes of kneading), place the dough ball into a large oiled bowl, cover with a tea towel, and let rise in a warm place for about an hour or until the dough has almost doubled in size.

5. Transfer the dough to a floured surface and roll into a 10 x 14-inch rectangle.

6. Make the filling: Combine the brown sugar, cinnamon, and salt in a small bowl. Using a pastry brush, brush the melted butter over the entire surface of the dough. Sprinkle the cinnamon-sugar mixture over the butter, using your fingers to lightly press the mixture into the dough. Starting with the longer side, roll up the dough to form a 14-inch cylinder. Gently cut the cylinder into 10 even rolls, using a serrated knife. Place in the prepared pan, cut side up. Cover and let rise in a warm place for about 45 to 60 minutes or until doubled.

7. Preheat the toaster oven to 350°F. Bake for 16 to 18 minutes or until slightly brown on top. Remove from the oven and place on a wire rack.

8. Meanwhile, make the glaze: Whisk the confectioners' sugar, 1 tablespoon milk, the coffee, vanilla, and butter in a medium bowl. If needed, whisk in the additional milk to make the desired consistency. Drizzle over the warm rolls.

Cinnamon Swirl Bread

MAKES 1 (9 X 5-INCH) LOAF

2 cups all-purpose flour

1 cup granulated sugar

1 teaspoon baking soda

½ teaspoon table salt

1 teaspoon cider vinegar

1 cup whole milk

1 large egg

¼ cup canola or vegetable oil

FILLING

½ cup granulated sugar

1 tablespoon ground
  cinnamon

GLAZE

¼ cup confectioners' sugar

2 teaspoons whole milk

CONVECTION OVEN VARIATION: Prepare the recipe as directed. Bake on the Convection Oven setting at 350°F for 35 to 40 minutes, or until a wooden pick inserted into the center comes out clean. Proceed as the recipe directs.

We worked on this book during a pandemic. Neither of us have ever experienced the changes in our everyday lives as we experienced during this time. Roxanne's family was working from home every day. New routines and rituals began during this time. One that was special was the 3:00 p.m. coffee break. Of course, no coffee break is complete without a sweet treat. Yeast was impossible to find during those difficult days, so this recipe was created for one such special family coffee moment. It comes together quickly and is delicious with or without coffee.

1. Preheat the toaster oven to 350°F. Grease the bottom of a 9 x 5-inch loaf pan.

2. Combine the flour, granulated sugar, baking soda, and salt in a large bowl. Place the vinegar in a 1-cup liquid measuring cup and add the milk; stir to combine. Whisk the milk mixture, egg, and oil in a medium bowl. Stir into the flour mixture, blending until combined.

3. Make the filling: Combine the granulated sugar and cinnamon in a small bowl.

4. Pour half of the batter into the prepared pan. Sprinkle half the cinnamon-sugar mixture over the batter in the loaf pan. Top with the remaining batter and sprinkle with remaining cinnamon-sugar mixture. Using a butter knife, make deep swirls in the batter. Make sure most of the cinnamon-sugar mixture from the top is covered in batter.

5. Bake for 45 to 50 minutes, or until a wooden pick inserted into the center comes out clean. Cool on a wire rack for 10 minutes. Run a knife around the edges of the bread, then remove the bread from the pan. Cool for an additional 10 minutes.

6. Meanwhile, make the glaze: Whisk the confectioners' sugar and milk in a small bowl until smooth. Drizzle the glaze over the partially cooled loaf. Serve warm or at room temperature.

Danish Pecan Pastry

SERVES 9

Are you anticipating overnight guests and want their stay to be special, or would you like to make your family feel like royalty? This is the recipe to satisfy both scenarios. Folks will think you spent hours on this pastry (secret: you won't). It is always a good idea to serve this with a piping hot cup of coffee.

1. Preheat the toaster oven to 375°F. Grease an 8 x 8-inch square baking pan.

2. Place the crescent roll dough on a lightly floured surface. Pinch the perforations together. Cut the dough in half to form two squares. Press one half of the dough into the bottom of the prepared pan.

3. Beat the cream cheese, brown sugar, egg, vanilla, and maple syrup in a large bowl using a handheld mixer, at medium-high speed, until smooth. Stir in the pecans. Spread evenly over the dough in the baking pan. Top with the remaining dough. Bake for 25 to 35 minutes. Let the pastry cool slightly.

4. Meanwhile, make the glaze: Whisk the confectioners' sugar, milk, and maple syrup in a small bowl. Drizzle over the pastry. Sprinkle with the ¼ cup pecans. Refrigerate any leftovers.

TIP: Toasting nuts intensifies their flavor and is easy to do in your toaster oven. See page 13.

1 (8-ounce) can refrigerated crescent roll dough

1 (8-ounce) package cream cheese, softened

½ cup packed dark brown sugar

1 large egg

½ teaspoon pure vanilla extract

1 tablespoon maple syrup

½ chopped pecans, toasted (see tip)

GLAZE

1 cup confectioners' sugar

1 tablespoon whole milk

1 tablespoon maple syrup

¼ cup chopped pecans, toasted

CONVECTION OVEN VARIATION: Prepare the recipe as directed. Bake on the Convection Oven setting at 375°F for 20 to 25 minutes. Proceed as the recipe directs.

Southern-Style Biscuits

MAKES 10

Once you have made Southern-style biscuits, you will never, ever go back to the canned spongy version from the supermarket. They can be made in a snap, and their flavor and texture make them a blue ribbon winner.

1. Preheat the toaster oven to 450°F.

2. Combine the flour, baking powder, and salt in a large bowl. Using a pastry cutter or two knives, cut the butter into the flour mixture until the mixture is crumbly throughout. Pour in the buttermilk and gently mix until just combined.

3. Turn the dough onto a lightly floured surface and knead lightly about 8 times. Roll the dough, using a rolling pin, until about ½ inch thick. Cut out rounds using a 2½-inch cutter. Place on an ungreased 12 x 12-inch baking pan or 8-inch round pan.

4. Bake for 10 to 12 minutes or until golden brown. Let cool slightly before serving warm.

TIPS: When cutting the dough, cut straight down and do not twist the cutter to help with an even rise while baking.

If biscuits are placed apart on the baking sheet, the sides will be crisp. If baked together in a round pan, the sides will be soft.

2 cups all-purpose flour

1 tablespoon baking powder

1 teaspoon table salt

4 tablespoons cold, unsalted butter, cut into bits

¾ to 1 cup buttermilk

CONVECTION OVEN VARIATION: Prepare the recipe as directed. Bake on the Convection Oven setting at 450°F for 8 to 10 minutes.

Bacon Cheddar Biscuits

MAKES 6

1 cup all-purpose flour

1 tablespoon baking powder

¼ teaspoon table salt

¼ teaspoon smoked paprika or freshly ground black pepper

3 tablespoons unsalted butter

½ cup whole milk

1 cup shredded sharp cheddar cheese

2 tablespoons minced fresh chives

4 slices bacon, cooked until crisp and crumbled

CONVECTION OVEN VARIATION: Prepare the recipe as directed. Bake on the Convection Oven setting at 425°F for 10 to 13 minutes.

These biscuits take on a delectable flavor thanks to the addition of crisp bacon, cheese, and chives. Serve them with soup or salad and lunch becomes memorable. They are also delicious split and topped with a spread of whipped garlic-herb cream cheese, then topped with slices of ham as a hearty sandwich.

1. Preheat the toaster oven to 425°F.

2. Stir the flour, baking powder, salt, and paprika in a large bowl. Using a pastry cutter or two knives, cut the butter into the flour mixture until the mixture is crumbly throughout. Pour in the milk and gently mix until just combined. Stir in the cheese, chives, and bacon.

3. Turn the dough onto a lightly floured surface and knead lightly about 8 times. Roll the dough, using a rolling pin, until about ¾ inch thick. Cut out rounds using a 2-inch cutter. Place 1 inch apart on an ungreased 12 x 12-inch baking pan. Bake for 12 to 15 minutes or until golden brown.

Espresso Chip Muffins

MAKES 6

Muffins add a delightful homemade touch to breakfast. In addition, who doesn't enjoy a muffin as a snack or with a cup of tea or coffee? Children and adults will both undoubtedly enjoy these bites of goodness filled with chocolate bits.

1. Preheat the toaster oven to 375°F. Grease a 6-cup muffin pan.

2. Whisk the flour, brown sugar, baking powder, espresso, salt, and cinnamon in a medium bowl. Combine the milk, butter, egg, and vanilla in a small bowl until blended. Make a well in the center of the flour mixture and add the milk mixture. Stir until just combined. Fold in the chocolate chips.

3. Spoon the batter evenly into the prepared muffin cups. Bake for 18 to 20 minutes, or until a wooden pick inserted into the center comes out clean. Cool on a wire rack for 5 minutes, then remove the muffins from the pan to finish cooling on a wire rack. Serve warm or at room temperature. Store in an airtight container.

1 cup all-purpose flour

6 tablespoons packed dark brown sugar

1¼ teaspoons baking powder

1 teaspoon instant espresso coffee powder

¼ teaspoon table salt

¼ teaspoon ground cinnamon

½ cup whole milk

¼ cup unsalted butter, melted and cooled slightly

1 large egg

½ teaspoon pure vanilla extract

½ cup mini semisweet chocolate chips

CONVECTION OVEN VARIATION: Prepare the recipe as directed. Bake on the Convection Oven setting at 375°F for 16 to 18 minutes, or until a wooden pick inserted into the center comes out clean. Proceed as the recipe directs.

Lemon Blueberry Scones

MAKES 6

1½ cups all-purpose flour

2 tablespoons granulated sugar

2¼ teaspoons baking powder

1 teaspoon grated lemon zest

¼ teaspoon table salt

¼ cup unsalted butter, cut into 1-tablespoon pieces

¾ cup fresh or frozen blueberries

¾ cup plus 1 tablespoon heavy cream, plus more for brushing

Coarse white sugar

LEMON GLAZE

1 cup confectioners' sugar

2 to 3 tablespoons fresh lemon juice

CONVECTION OVEN VARIATION: Prepare the recipe as directed. Bake on the Convection Oven setting at 400°F for 17 to 22 minutes or until golden brown. Proceed as the recipe directs.

We often teach cooking classes, and one of our most popular classes showcases how to host a tea for Mother's Day, a shower, a holiday celebration, or anytime friends gather for a relaxing time to chat. We pattern the refreshments and tea service after an elegant afternoon English tea. Of course, we always serve scones, for it wouldn't be tea without them.

1. Line a 12 x 12-inch baking pan with parchment paper.

2. Whisk the flour, granulated sugar, baking powder, lemon zest, and salt in a large bowl. Cut in the butter using a pastry cutter or two knives until the mixture is crumbly throughout. Gently stir in the blueberries, taking care not to mash them. Add ¾ cup cream and gently stir until a soft dough forms. If needed, stir in an additional tablespoon of cream so all of the flour is moistened.

3. Turn the dough onto a lightly floured board. Pat the dough into a circle about ¾ inch thick and 6 inches in diameter. Cut into 6 triangles. Arrange the triangles on the prepared pan. Freeze for 15 minutes.

4. Preheat the toaster oven to 400°F. Brush the scones lightly with cream and sprinkle with coarse sugar. Bake for 20 to 25 minutes or until golden brown. Let cool for 5 minutes.

5. Meanwhile, make the glaze: Stir the confectioners' sugar and lemon juice in a small bowl, blending until smooth. Drizzle the glaze over the scones. Let stand for about 5 minutes. These taste best served freshly made and slightly warm.

Chili Cheese Cornbread

MAKES 1 (9-INCH) CORNBREAD

Nonstick cooking spray

¾ cup yellow cornmeal

¾ cup all-purpose flour

¼ cup sugar

1¾ teaspoons baking powder

½ teaspoon baking soda

½ teaspoon table salt

½ teaspoon chili powder

½ cup sour cream

½ cup buttermilk

2 large eggs

3 tablespoons unsalted butter, melted and cooled slightly

1 tablespoon canola or vegetable oil

1¼ cups shredded sharp cheddar cheese

1 cup frozen corn, partially thawed

1 (4-ounce) can chopped green chilies

CONVECTION OVEN VARIATION: Prepare the recipe as directed. Bake on the Convection Oven setting at 425°F for 12 to 17 minutes, or until a wooden pick inserted into the center comes out clean. Proceed as the recipe directs.

This cornbread becomes something extraordinary with the addition of green chilies, cheese, and corn. Who can resist? Cut a big piece anytime, but especially when serving chili.

1. Preheat the toaster oven to 425°F. Spray a 9-inch round cake pan with nonstick cooking spray.

2. Whisk the cornmeal, flour, sugar, baking powder, baking soda, salt, and chili powder in a large bowl.

3. Whisk the sour cream, buttermilk, eggs, melted butter, and oil in a small bowl. Pour the wet ingredients into the dry ingredients and stir until completely combined. Stir in the cheese, corn, and green chilies.

4. Pour the batter into the prepared pan. Bake for 15 to 20 minutes, or until a wooden pick inserted into the center comes out clean. Let cool for 5 minutes. Cut into wedges and serve warm.

TIP: Are you out of buttermilk? Pour 1½ teaspoons white vinegar or lemon juice into a 1-cup liquid measuring cup and add milk to equal ½ cup. Let stand for a few minutes, then use it for this recipe.

VARIATION: This recipe is also delicious as a classic homestyle cornbread. Just omit the chili powder, cheese, corn, and green chilies. Prepare and bake as directed above. And for an extra-special presentation, serve with a spread of your own honey butter. To make the honey butter, blend ½ cup softened butter with 1 to 2 tablespoons honey and a dash of kosher salt.

Buttered Poppy Seed Bread

MAKES 1 (9 X 5-INCH) LOAF

Get ready for hot and inviting dinner bread, without spending more than a few minutes in the kitchen. The day before you plan to serve it, brush a loaf of frozen bread dough with the herb-seasoned butter. Place it in the refrigerator overnight, then let it stand at room temperature to finish thawing and to let it rise. All that is left is to pop it into the oven.

3 tablespoons unsalted butter, melted

1 (1-pound) loaf frozen white bread dough

1 teaspoon poppy seeds

¼ teaspoon onion powder

¼ teaspoon garlic powder

¼ teaspoon freshly ground black pepper

1. Pour about half of the melted butter into a 9 x 5-inch loaf pan. Brush the butter to cover the sides and bottom of the pan. Place the frozen bread loaf in the pan. Brush the top of the loaf with the remaining butter, covering completely. Stir the poppy seeds, onion powder, garlic powder, and pepper in a small bowl. Sprinkle the seasonings over the top of the bread. Cover with plastic wrap and refrigerate overnight.

2. Remove the bread from the refrigerator and loosen the plastic wrap so it is loosely covered. Let it rise at room temperature until the top of the bread is just over the top edge of the pan, about 2 to 4 hours.

3. Preheat the toaster oven to 350°F.

4. Bake for 20 to 25 minutes or until the bread is golden brown.

5. Let cool for 5 minutes, then remove the loaf from the pan and place on a wire rack to cool for a few minutes. Slice and serve warm.

VARIATION: Substitute sesame seeds for the poppy seeds, if desired. Or, for "everything bread," combine both sesame seeds and poppy seeds with the remaining seasonings.

CONVECTION OVEN VARIATION: Prepare the recipe as directed. Bake on the Convection Oven setting at 350°F for 18 to 23 minutes or until golden brown. Proceed as the recipe directs.

Garlic Cheese Pull-Apart Bread

Transform a loaf of frozen bread dough into a warm, inviting bread laced with garlic, butter, and cheese. Everyone at the dinner table will be asking for more.

1. Rub the frozen dough lightly with the oil. Place it in a zip-top bag and refrigerate overnight to thaw.

2. Spray a 9 x 5-inch loaf pan with nonstick cooking spray.

3. Stir the butter, garlic, parsley, salt, and pepper in a small bowl; set aside.

4. Place the thawed dough on a lightly floured board and roll into a 12-inch square. Brush about 3 tablespoons of the butter mixture over the top of the dough. Sprinkle evenly with about ½ cup Parmesan and ½ cup mozzarella. Roll the dough over the filling, jelly-roll style. Cut into rolls ½ to ¾ inch thick. Stand the rolls upright in the loaf pan, two across, with the cut side of the rolls facing the narrow end of the pan. (There will be two rows, side by side, with 8 to 10 rolls in each row.) Cover with a towel and let rise for about 1 hour.

5. Preheat the toaster oven to 350°F. Bake for 18 to 23 minutes, or until the loaf is golden brown. Drizzle with the remaining melted butter mixture. Sprinkle with the remaining 2 tablespoons Parmesan cheese and the remaining ¼ cup mozzarella cheese. Bake for 2 to 3 minutes for the cheese to melt.

6. Place the pan on a wire rack and let stand for 5 minutes. Remove the loaf from the pan. Serve warm.

1 (1-pound) loaf frozen white bread dough

Canola or vegetable oil

Nonstick cooking spray

6 tablespoons unsalted butter, melted

3 cloves garlic, finely minced

2 tablespoons minced fresh flat-leaf (Italian) parsley

¼ teaspoon table salt

¼ teaspoon freshly ground black pepper

⅔ cup shredded Parmesan cheese

¾ cup shredded mozzarella cheese

CONVECTION OVEN SETTING: Prepare the recipe as directed. Bake on the Convection Oven setting at 350°F for 15 to 20 minutes or until golden brown. Top with the remaining butter, Parmesan and mozzarella cheeses and bake for 2 to 3 minutes for the cheese to melt. Proceed as the recipe directs.

Metric Charts

The recipes that appear in this cookbook use the standard US method for measuring liquid and dry or solid ingredients (teaspoons, tablespoons, and cups). The information on these pages is provided to help cooks outside the United States successfully use these recipes. All equivalents are approximate.

Metric Equivalents for Different Types of Ingredients

A standard cup measure of a dry or solid ingredient will vary in weight depending on the type of ingredient. A standard cup of liquid is the same volume for any type of liquid. Use the following chart when converting standard cup measures to grams (weight) or milliliters (volume).

STANDARD CUP	FINE POWDER (ex. flour)	GRAIN (ex. rice)	GRANULAR (ex. sugar)	LIQUID SOLIDS (ex. butter)	LIQUID (ex. milk)
1	140 g	150 g	190 g	200 g	240 ml
¾	105 g	113 g	143 g	150 g	180 ml
⅔	93 g	100 g	125 g	133 g	160 ml
½	70 g	75 g	95 g	100 g	120 ml
⅓	47 g	50 g	63 g	67 g	80 ml
¼	35 g	38 g	48 g	50 g	60 ml
⅛	18 g	19 g	24 g	25 g	30 ml

Useful Equivalents for Dry Ingredients by Weight

(To convert ounces to grams, multiply the number of ounces by 30.)

OZ	LB	G
1 oz	¹⁄₁₆ lb	30 g
4 oz	¼ lb	120 g
8 oz	½ lb	240 g
12 oz	¾ lb	360 g
16 oz	1 lb	480 g

Useful Equivalents for Length

(To convert inches to centimeters, multiply the number of inches by 2.5.)

IN	FT	YD	CM	M
1 in			2.5 cm	
6 in	½ ft		15 cm	
12 in	1 ft		30 cm	
36 in	3 ft	1 yd	90 cm	
40 in			100 cm	1 m

Useful Equivalents for Liquid Ingredients by Volume

TSP	TBSP	CUPS	FL OZ	ML	L
¼ tsp				1 ml	
½ tsp				2 ml	
1 tsp				5 ml	
3 tsp	1 Tbsp		½ fl oz	15 ml	
	2 Tbsp	⅛ cup	1 fl oz	30 ml	
	4 Tbsp	¼ cup	2 fl oz	60 ml	
	5⅓ Tbsp	⅓ cup	3 fl oz	80 ml	
	8 Tbsp	½ cup	4 fl oz	120 ml	
	10⅔ Tbsp	⅔ cup	5 fl oz	160 ml	
	12 Tbsp	¾ cup	6 fl oz	180 ml	
	16 Tbsp	1 cup	8 fl oz	240 ml	
	1 pt	2 cups	16 fl oz	480 ml	
	1 qt	4 cups	32 fl oz	960 ml	
			33 fl oz	1000 ml	1 L

Useful Equivalents for Cooking/Oven Temperatures

	FAHRENHEIT	CELSIUS	GAS MARK
FREEZE WATER	32°F	0°C	
ROOM TEMPERATURE	68°F	20°C	
BOIL WATER	212°F	100°C	
	325°F	160°C	3
	350°F	180°C	4
	375°F	190°C	5
	400°F	200°C	6
	425°F	220°C	7
	450°F	230°C	8
BROIL			Grill

Acknowledgments

Way back in middle school, we both knew we wanted a career working with food. When that happened, we then dreamed of writing a cookbook. We had written thousands of recipes for companies, but we longed to write a cookbook with our names listed as the authors. Dreams do come true, and in our case, many times over, for which we are so grateful. Each time we write a book, we pinch ourselves and remember what an honor it is to share our passion for cooking with you, our readers.

We appreciate our friends and all those who help us on our way. First, let us begin with our friendship. It is wonderful to work with your best friend. That chance meeting many years ago in the test kitchen for a small appliance company led to a deep and lasting friendship. We are grateful we can work together, laugh together, and continue to support each other.

Roxanne

The excitement of writing a cookbook always causes my heart to swell and creates a huge smile. I can't imagine a better gift than writing and sharing my love for cooking. It is always a blessing to work on the idea, concepts, and testing, and compiling all the information that Kathy and I want to share in a cookbook. After more than three decades of working together, I would be remiss not to share my love and appreciation for my business partner and compadre in all things food. Thank you, Kathy Moore, for your heart and soul that you pour into our business every day and the love that you have shared with me from day one.

We wrote this book during the 2020 pandemic. My husband, Bob Bateman, and my daughter, Grace, were home with me as I created and crafted each recipe. They are always supportive, but this time it was different. The three of us formed a bond and a circle around this book, and for that I am truly grateful. This is the first time ever that my family was by my side each step of the way in the cookbook process. They tasted and offered wise counsel on the recipes. Bob came to the kitchen when he heard the water running and picked up the kitchen towel to help me with the dishes. Together we enjoyed meal after meal, all of which were prepared in the toaster oven, perfect for a family of three. Most nights, Grace would exclaim several times, "Mom, promise you will make this one again!" That is her very own way of giving a recipe five stars. My family is my circle, my team, and my cheering squad. These pandemic days we shared were sad for so many and caused us great anxiety, but the gift of time with my family during this creative process will remain stamped on my heart forever. The best part of any day is always the time the three of us share around the table. I love you more than words can tell. Thank you.

Kathy

My husband, David, and daughters, Laura and Amanda, mean everything to me and I love them more than words can express. I appreciate their constant support, their patience answering yet another tech question, and genuine willingness to help in the kitchen or taste another recipe. Their laughter and smiles bring joy into my world. Thank you for encouraging me and sharing all of life with me.

Friends come into our lives and are a true blessing. God blessed me with the most incredible friend decades ago when I met Roxanne Wyss. Friendship for us takes on a richer, deeper meaning, since we are both friends and business partners. It is wonderful beyond dreams to share our passion for food, teaching, and writing cookbooks. We have grown over time, and perhaps few duos have ever shared as many adventures, laughs, and new projects as we have. At the same time, we have turned to each other for support in all of those challenging times when only a friend, and someone you love and trust, can help. Thank you for everything and thank God for you.

Roxanne + Kathy

A cookbook is the result of many people working together and we appreciate each of you.

Thank you to Lisa and Sally Ekus, our agents and our friends. We thank you and your entire team for all you do to guide and support us on this journey.

Thank you to Anja Schmidt and everyone at Tiller and Simon & Schuster for creating such great books. Your careful attention to detail and hard work shows in the quality of the books. We are thrilled and honored to work with you.

And we want to thank each of you. Our career is seasoned with wonderful people—friends we make as we teach classes, those we meet when writing articles, those we work with—both lifelong friends and newly minted ones. We have become friends with many of you through our blog, pluggedintocooking.com, and we enjoy that connection. The people and all the friendships we make are so important to us. Thank you.

Index

Page numbers in *italics* refer to illustrations.

About the Authors

ROXANNE WYSS + KATHY MOORE are cookbook authors, food consultants, food writers, cooking teachers, and food bloggers who share their test-kitchen expertise through creative recipes and tips that make cooking easier and more fun. This is their seventeenth cookbook; recent titles include *The Easy Air Fryer Cookbook* and *Instant & Healthy: 100 Low-Fuss, High-Flavor Recipes for Your Pressure Cooker, Multicooker & Instant Pot*, in addition to baking books, including *Delicious Bundt Cakes, Delicious Poke Cakes,* and *Delicious Dump Cakes.* They teach cooking classes, consult with food and appliance companies, write feature articles, and appear on national television, including QVC. Their professional careers in food began in a test kitchen for a small appliance company and now span over thirty years. Their popular food blog can be found at www.pluggedintocooking.com.